The World Is a Reflection of the Mind

Xuemo

Translated by J. C. Cleary

中国大百科全书出版社
Encyclopedia of China Publishing House

First Edition 2018

ISBN 978-7-5202-0273-2

Copyright © 2018 by Xuemo

Published by Encyclopedia of China Publishing House

Fuchengmen Beidajie No.17, Xicheng District , Beijing, China

Tel:(86)10-88390739

http://www.ecph.com.cn

E-mail:limoyun2008@sina.com

Printed by October Printing Ltd., Company

Contents

Preface

"The World Is a Reflection of the Mind" is an insight of wisdom. In traditional cultivation, only those whose cultivation and realization reach the highest level are able to have this kind of wisdom and level of perception. Only those who truly understand this principle will easily merge with "the yoga apart from sophistry," and truly manifest what we often call "illuminating mind and seeing its true nature."

For those people who are constantly troubled by pain and suffering, this book has a wondrous function that other books cannot replace. When our whole community has fallen into affliction and anxiety, it is without doubt a dose of the good medicine of wisdom.

In the Buddhist sutras there is a verse that goes like this: "If people want to completely understand all the buddhas of the past, present, and future, they must observe the true nature of the phenomenal realm, that everything is only a creation of the mind."

This is the primal source of the wisdom of the present book. But talk is talk, and action is action: sometimes understanding at the level of "truth" cannot represent a firm grasp at the level of "things and events." So the existence of the present book has its value.

This book is a vivid exposition of worldly phenomena for the world-transcending wisdom of Buddhism. Since it is the vision and viewpoint of wisdom, it also has many ways of making close connections with real life. Since it can alter our "minds," it can also change our "actions," and then it can change our "lives." Many people, because of the ignorance of the "mind," are ignorant in "action" and they end up having many difficulties in "life" and die an untimely death. It is just as it says in my novel *Desert Hunters*: "When the mind is illuminated, the road opens up." It is precisely because their minds rise to a higher level and wisdom appears, many people who were originally mired in difficulties at last realize transcendence, and become people of accomplishment in our eyes. We can pick out this kind of inspiration among many illustrious names, such as Steve Jobs, who benefited from Zen. And Zen, in the system of the Great Mudra, is the Great Mudra of the Mark of Reality. From the Zen viewpoint, even the shadow of death cannot cover the creative wisdom of Steve Jobs, and we now still get to enjoy the series of Apple products he left behind.

Thus I have often said: "Life is created by the mind. Your life is a reflection of your mind. The world that appears in your eyes is also a reflection of your mind. Whatever kind of mind you have, you will have that kind of life. Whatever kind of mind you have, you will also have that kind of world. Only when your mind goes from small to large, will your world go from small to large. Without a change of mind, it is definitely impossible to have a change in your life. Therefore, you can also call this book 'a prescription for building a life.'"

Around me there are many people who have changed their lives and fates by relying on the wisdom of this book. Among them are people suffering from fatal illnesses, those with serious depression, those who did not want to go on living after the deaths of people they were close to, those who had lost hope and were sick of the world. Many of them, after coming into contact with my writings, through a change of their minds, had their lives elevated to a higher level. Thus, some friends hoped that I would be able to take this kind of wisdom and communicate it in popular form, without religious trappings, and in this way produce a book that enables people who do not necessarily have religious beliefs to detach from suffering and attain happiness.

The wisdom in this book has its source in traditional Great Mudra Buddhism, and the author is a follower of the Shangpa Kagyu Great Mudra. In my book *The Great Mudra of Light: The Heart of Real Practice* (published by Central Compilation & Translation Press), I concentrated on introducing the Shangpa Kagyu School's Five Diamond Teachings of Niguma. In its procedure for completing (the mind of enlightenment) there is "the method of the three branches." What it conveys is the wisdom of the present book:

"The excellent understanding of the Path of the Master Teacher is understanding that all appearances are the Master Teacher, understanding that the nature of the inherent mind is the empty inherent nature, and thus achieving a definitive perception.

"The excellent understanding of the Fundamental Buddha is that all appearances are Buddha Father and Buddha Mother — they appear but have no inherent nature. (It is) understanding that all that appears and all that is heard is the inherent mind, and the nature of the inherent mind is the empty inherent nature, and achieving a definitive perception.

"The path of (knowing that all things) are like an illusion is definitively knowing that all appearances and thoughts are the inherent mind, and definitively knowing that the inherent mind is illusory transformation. If we investigate the inherent nature of the six sense faculties and the corresponding six sense objects, then we see that their inherent nature is empty, yet can manifest appearances; apparent manifestations are not different from emptiness; apparent manifestations have no inherent nature, and are like illusory transformations. If we eliminate clinging and attachment to discriminating thought, then amidst manifestations and emptiness without clinging, we enter into profound meditative concentration."

The present book is an explanation and elucidation of this

ancient wisdom in everyday language. It is detached from names and forms, and directly points to the human mind, with the power to penetrate the human mind.

We must recognize that clinging and attachments are the source of pain and suffering, and if we have no clinging and attachments, then we will have no pain and suffering. But often what we cling to and feel attached to are just concepts and illusions.

We must know that everything before our eyes will ultimately disappear. Countless material things, countless wealth, countless people, countless complications, will all be dissolved away by the waters of time until no trace of them remains; they will all dissolve away into the eternal dark night like bursting bubbles.

Our past, our present, and our future will all become memories. But our memories too are being swallowed up in the maw of forgetting. The ones we are able to force ourselves to keep are bits of memories like dreams or illusions.

Many times, our memories and our current understanding of those memories determine our present and our future.

The only thing we can hold onto is our own minds. Our minds determine our present moment. What we can hold onto is just the present moment.

Because of the changing basic substance of time and the myriad things, nothing we have can avoid "birth, old age, sickness, and death." Thus, the basic substance of the world is suffering—

this is the meaning of the Buddhist concept that "all defiled phenomena entail suffering." But because human life entails suffering, we must have the spirit that will enable our "bliss" — this is the meaning of the worldly teaching of Buddhism. When we realize this point, we can liberate ourselves from suffering, and enter into pure bliss, and thereby realize the freedom of the world-transcending meaning of the Buddhist Teaching. The bliss of worldly phenomena is conditional; the bliss of the world-transcending is unconditional. The bliss of the latter is in fact the breaking up of clingings and the transcendence that comes after we discover the true characteristic of phenomena.

This true characteristic of phenomena is the subject matter of this book, and is revealed by the title of this book: The World Is a Reflection of the Mind.

When we genuinely read and understand this book, when we can achieve wondrous functioning, then we will truly be able to "detach from suffering and attain bliss."

First Series:

The Immutable True Characteristic

There Is Nothing in the World That Can Last Forever

Whether it is beautiful or it is ugly, whether you have it or you lose it, in the world there is nothing that can exist forever, nor can any situation exist forever. The world is this way. Everything in the world is a big false appearance. Why do we say these things are false appearances? Because they cannot last forever, but they let you think they will always be this way. This error we call "accepting the false as true."

If you have not entered deeply into a complete understanding of Buddhist wisdom, the principle that "all contrived things are like dreams, like illusions, like bubbles, like reflections" will surely make you feel confused, it will seem inconceivable, and you might more or less reject it. I can understand this. Ultimately you can see and touch these cars and these apartment buildings and so on—they are the entirety of our lives. These things that are so real—how can they become like dreams, like illusions, like bubbles, like reflections? That's a good question. In reality, Buddhists do not deny this reality of theirs, but they emphasize that their existence is an apparent existence. They are temporary, and they cannot last forever.

Everything in the world is in a process of uninterrupted change. Some changes can influence the surface appearance of things, and you can see them clearly, but some changes are very subtle, and take place inside things. They are like hypocrites in the community, weaving together lies that people enjoy hearing and seeing, to the point that many intelligent people are taken in by them.

Let me bring up a simple example: a beautiful girl enjoys her own beauty, and many boys are captivated by her beautiful appearance, but this kind of beautiful appearance will not last forever. The girl will always develop white hair, wrinkles, and will inevitably show signs of old age, not to mention the subtle changes in her body, the sudden birth and death of cells, the constantly changing thoughts. What's more, she is the same as the ordinary looking women: she has dirty inside her body, her skin is covered with bacteria, her body is supported by bones. But the girls themselves are not conscious of this: they jealously vie with other beautiful girls for male attention in a life-or-death struggle. But they do not understand that beauty seized by the mind of suffering will always be taken away by time.

In fact, whether it is beautiful or it is ugly, whether you have it or you lose it, in the world there is nothing that can exist forever, nor can any situation exist forever. The world is this way.

Everything in the world is a big false appearance. Why do we say these things are false appearances? Because they cannot last forever, but they let you think they will always be this way. This error we call "accepting the false as true."

The myriad things do not have an eternal changeless intrinsic nature: they have no self, they are impermanent, but after the causal conditions come together, they can manifest various kinds of apparent forms. The external world which we see is a coming together of causal conditions, so of course it returns to the empty inherent nature, and it is impermanent. Moreover, many times what we see is not the true face of things and events: it is only the manifestation of our own minds. This is the meaning of the saying "the myriad phenomena are only fabrications of the mind." For example, for a beggar out in the cold, having clothes to wear and food to eat is heaven. If one day this beggar becomes a rich man, then for him his heaven will be some other situation. This is the way it is.

So then, ultimately, are there any things that really exist, or not? There are, but their existence is "existence through causal origination." For example, the cup we use to drink water does not have a fundamental essence that can last forever without changing, so we term it "empty." But this is not to say that this cup is not there. Up until now, the cup still exists, but it does not have an eternal unchanging fundamental essence. They really exist, but they are also temporary appearances. This is because, in the next moment the situation may change into something that is not the same. Change is the true characteristic of this world, and no matter how you reject it, you will still constantly encounter it.

A young friend told me a story: She had been a very insecure person, afraid of the unknown, always wanting to control everything around her. One day her young husband suddenly died. Three hours before her husband died, the two of them had talked over the phone. Having experienced this event, she finally discovered that all she could truly control was her own mind. She said to me that she and her husband had originally agreed that the next month they would go on their honeymoon, and she would have her picture taken in her wedding dress, and the month after that they wanted to conceive a child, and after two years they would return to the husband's hometown for the child to grow up. But all of this turned into a dream.

Everything is fundamentally a dream. Her husband's existence was a dream, and some years later, her own existence would also become a dream. Is there anything that we must be concerned about, anything that we can be concerned about? When you truly understand the impermanence of worldly things, you will understand this statement. Luckily, what change brings is not all pain and suffering and helplessness: it also implies that all pain, suffering and helplessness will pass.

That friend also told me that in the first month after her husband died, it was as if she were living in hell, and every day she dreaded waking up, and every day she longed to be reunited with her husband in dreams. It was as if her mind was burning in the karmic fire, while her body was freezing in an icehouse. She said that every day she was waiting in a cold lonely room, not seeing any friends, not eating, as if her whole human form was bled dry. But this painful suffering did disappear. She ended up understanding that everything in the world is all like a dewdrop in the sunshine: in the twinkling of an eye it can evaporate, and nothing can last forever.

My younger brother died when he was twenty-seven. Friends who have read my book *Desert Rites* all know that for me at that time, his death was without doubt a deadly blow, but at the same time, it smashed my illusions about life, and broke up many of my clingings and attachments. Not long after it happened, I came to a thorough understanding of what the true characteristic of the world is. I knew that whether you cling to it or not, the world is always in the midst of change. The bright morning will always go into the dark night, and the dark night will always welcome the dawn. Children will slowly grow up, and parents will gradually grow old. All the stories in human life, whether we live through them ourselves, or hear about them from others, will all vanish in an instant, like a splash of water in our memories, or a flash of lightning in the night sky.

Every experience, every event, every thing, every person—all these are apparent phenomena, and they will not endure forever, and they do not have fixed identities. Whether good or bad, they all just exist in our interpretation here and now. Thus we say: why must we take every experience and view it as so real? Why must we care about these ceaselessly changing appearances? Holding onto the present moment, savoring the present moment, enjoying the present moment, drawing nourishment from the present moment, letting the past go into the past, keeping the future in the future — this alone is a healthy attitude for living.

There Is No Way to Resist Impermanence, But It Should Not Be Feared

Everything in the world, when we investigate its fundamental root, will become a memory. There is no duality between memory and illusion, so we say, life is one giant illusion. When you are happy, the world is changing, and you yourself are changing. When you are suffering, this change will not stop for a moment because of your suffering. Impermanence is the precondition for life being able to continue, and it is also the rule that we ourselves always follow. Impermanence itself should not be feared.

People are vey interesting, because most people just want to accept the enjoyable aspect of things, and are always subconsciously avoiding the aspect that is not enjoyable. Thus, they are never willing to calmly accept the results that are brought on by their choices.

Let's take a simple example. Many men like to take their wives and children out to have fun, but when they encounter traffic jams and have to stand in queues, they are always full of complaints. Many boys like pretty girls, but when one of these girls becomes their girlfriend, they are afraid she will receive favors from other men. There are truly countless examples like this in life.

So what does this mean? It means that we cannot clearly see the true face of things, because our one-sided views block our line of sight. That is why we resist impermanence in this way. In fact, impermanence is a natural law. The only difference between the two is that you can avoid eating sweets, but there is no way for you to resist change.

You will also discover that your own fear of "the unknown" is linked to a kind of resistance to "change." The great majority of people like stable certainty, they like everything to continue in its original condition. Any possibility of "loss" will make us shudder. However, except for making yourself feel that things are unbearable, this kind of fear cannot accomplish much. This is because natural law is far stronger than an individual living being. Perhaps through certain methods we can try to slow down the process of change, but ultimately we have no way to block the emergence of change. But does this have some absolute relationship with happiness? When you are happy, the world is changing, and you yourself are changing. When you are suffering, this change will not stop for a moment because of your suffering. Impermanence is the precondition for life being able to continue, and it is also the rule that we ourselves always follow.

Impermanence itself should not be feared.

So then, why are we so fearful of the "unknown?" Because we accept the false as true, and we fear accepting the pain of loss, and we are never willing to let go of anything. But many times, you are unwilling to let go, but you have to let go. Again, once you calmly accept this "loss," you will discover that actually it is not so fearful as you imagined. Why? Because everything in the world, if we investigate its root, will all become memories, and memories are no different from illusions. That's why we say that life is one vast illusion.

Let's take an example. Does this apartment building where I live exist? Of course it exists. It can protect me and my family from the wind and rain; it can hold all the things I cherish: my books, my rock collection, my calligraphy, and so on. But it is not something that fundamentally exists, it is just an apparent phenomenon, and it has no eternally unchanging inherent nature. Years ago this plot of land was a cemetery. My grandfather built a small shed not far from here to collect manure, the manure from the railroad tracks. He took the manure and stored it in the house where he lived, and piled it on the ground, fearing people would steal it, and he ate and slept in that house. In his eyes, this manure was more important than anything, and could not be lost. But he did not understand that this manure was something formed by the coming together of causal conditions, and this house too was something formed by the coming together of causal conditions.

Years later, the house was torn down, and the cemetery was flattened, and crops were planted. More than ten years after that, the cropland became a farm, and people fought bloody battles for land to build houses on. These people did not know that this village was also something formed by the coming together of causal conditions. They also did not know that many years later, this piece of land would be bought by a big boss, and the village would be flattened, and made into an area of modernized dwelling units. Later, I bought one of the buildings, and came to live there. At that point, this empty house again filled up with my things. But this was not the end; it will still go on changing, and will go on ceaselessly changing. This is because, be it a village, a building, or some land, nothing has a basic substance that is eternally unchanging. Because of the coming together of causal conditions, they have had many apparent forms. We call this causal origination. But their basic substance is without inherent nature. They undergo changes all the time, and so they are also called inherently empty.

Everything in the world, after being born and maturing, will stay in a certain form for a period of time, and will later decay and perish and undergo illusory transformation and finally disappear. The inherent emptiness of causal origination is the law of how the world operates, and all things are like this. When you understand this point, and you go back and reflect again on everything in life, in your mind there will naturally be fewer delusions and emotions, and more lucidity and equanimity.

A friend told me that when she was in college, she had liked a certain young man, and was very fond of him. Later the two of them became closer and closer, and the young man became unwilling to be apart from her. But one day, she suddenly lost all her feelings for him, and later left his world without the least hesitation. Similar things happened many times, and she asked me if she were some kind of oddity. I told her she was not.

In reality, the love between a man and a woman is the lesser love: it is a feeling, an emotion. For it to develop, for it to stay fresh, certain conditions are required. When these conditions continually change, love may go through a process of being born, becoming ardent, cooling off, and perishing. For example, you love a woman because of her beauty; then when she is no longer beautiful, will you still love her? You love someone because you have the same ambitions and are on the same path; when you are no longer seeking the same things, will you still love him? You love a woman because she loves you; when she is no longer as fond of you as before, will your love for her still be the same as it was? You love a person because he understands you, but if he can no longer interpret you, will you still love him? The conditions that impel people to love each other are constantly changing, and that is why very few people can love each other their whole lives. With many lovers, after they have lived a long time, their love changes into a kind of familiar affection, or a kind of habit. What people who can continue hand-in-hand into old age rely upon is certainly not a kind of romantic but volatile feeling. What's more, even if people can love each other through their whole lifetimes, in the end they will still be separated by death. Thus, love cannot last forever.

So then, what does last forever? Impermanence. Impermanence alone is the world's eternal truth. However, this does not imply that you should treat love and human life casually. On the contrary, after you understand this point, you must liberate yourself from all the wounds of the past and all the unease about the future, and thoroughly appreciate and value every moment in life; you must no longer take great pains forcing yourself to search for a permanence that does not exist.

Flowing and Changing Causal Conditions Are the Mother of Change

Everything in the past, all time, is like flowing water. Days and nights flow along without stopping, and disappear. All things, all apparent forms, are like bubbles in water: those being born are being born, and those being extinguished are being extinguished. A batch of humans die off, and a batch of humans are born, birth and death, death and birth, like ripples of light on the surface of the water, endlessly shimmering.

If you have the habit of observing, you will certainly discover an interesting rule. What rule? You will not be able to find any material thing that exists independently, and you will not be able to find any happening that exists independently. In this world, there are no effects without causes and there are no causes without effects. Seeds that are buried in the ground perish prematurely, because they did not get the careful attention of the person doing the sowing. Those that died prematurely are no longer seeds, but become part of the nutrients in the soil.

The world constantly flows on like this, with one thing linked to another, endlessly cycling. Therefore, it is not as it superficially appears to be, composed of countless independent entities. Sometimes what seems to be an inadvertent choice may take the little boat of your life and lead it into a totally different harbor. People call this law "the domino effect" or "the butterfly effect." Buddhists call it "causal conditioning." The continuity of causal conditioning is the basis of the continuous flowing changes of life: it is precisely the causal conditioning that creates each and every transformation.

There is a song lyric that says: "If there is a causal connection, they will come a thousand miles to meet. If there is no causal connection, they can be face to face and it will be hard to join hands." This expresses the true characteristic of the world very well. What true characteristic? Everything in the world, reasonable or not, is the result of the coming together of causal conditions. Without the coming together of causal conditions, there would be no appearing of apparent forms. On the other hand, once causal conditions disintegrate, apparent forms disappear along with them. Moreover, this disappearing of an apparent form also implies the birth of another apparent form. This is because often it is the dissolution of one set of causal conditions that is the beginning of another set of causal conditions. This is the law of motion of the whole world. When we genuinely understand "causal conditions," we understand what impermanence is.

Let me give a simple example. If you do not like rainy weather, you will feel that when it rains it is troublesome, and it will bring you a lot of annoyances: your shoes will always get wet, and the clothes you have washed cannot dry. But if every day you are sharing an umbrella with your girlfriend and strolling along together in the rain, enjoying the romance of the rain, then you will surely not complain.

Thus we say that you should not care too much about anything in the world, because whether you care about it or not, everything will change sometime. What stands out may become mundane, what is ordinary may become great, what succeeds may fail, and what fails may succeed. How can there be anything certain in this world? Our emotions are always like waves in the wind: this one rises and that one falls. Our view of other people also constantly changes according to what we see and hear. Is there anything that will not pass? We must not twist and turn because we see adversity before us, and we must not be overjoyed because of some temporary favorable circumstances. Flowing changing causal conditions imply that there are too many possibilities in life. So we must keep lucidity and a sense of reverence.

You know that the result of every choice we make, of every action we take, becomes the causal basis for the next choice and the next action. The dewdrop evaporates in the sunshine, and turns into water vapor, and rises into the sky. On the original leaf of the tree there is no trace of it, while in the sky there is one more little bit of moisture. When countless bits of moisture encounter the cold air, they may turn into clouds, and if they happen to encounter the right conditions, they turn into rain, and return to the earth. This is the way it is. There is a momentary disjuncture in the cycling between cause and effect: this too is the basic reason why the changes in the world never cease. Thus we have the illusory awareness of the passage of time and we have memories replacing each other.

On a certain afternoon at dusk, you are standing on a balcony lit by the afterglow of the setting sun, and you remember little things from the past. You might feel that all of time is like flowing water. Days and nights flow along without stopping, and disappear. All things, all apparent forms, are like bubbles in water: those being born are being born, and those being extinguished are being extinguished. A batch of humans die off, and a batch of humans are born, birth and death, death and birth, like ripples of light on the surface of the water, ceaselessly shimmering.

In reality, the myriad things in the world are all this way. When you observe causal conditions, you must observe all kinds of apparent forms this way. If you are able to observe these apparent forms, it implies that you have developed a kind of wisdom. In Buddhism there is the teaching of the "twelve links of causation." It points out the twelve links from causal origination to causal extinction:

The first is ignorance: not knowing, stupidity; this is the

basic reason that people get trapped in the various kinds of causal conditions.

The second is action: whatever we say, whatever we do, whatever we think.

The third is consciousness: how we interpret external conditions; this is related to the mind of the individual person, and it feeds the seeds of action.

The fourth is name and form: set concepts and viewpoints and so on not related to the eyes, ears, nose, tongue, body, and conceptual mind.

The fifth is the six sense organs: we get information about the external world through the six sense faculties — eyes, ears, nose, tongue, body, and conceptual mind, and we use this to know the world.

The sixth is contact: awareness of contact, and the feelings that take shape instantaneously from contact.

The seventh is sensation: getting sensation, receiving certain feelings or certain results.

The eighth is craving: greedy desire, becoming besotted with certain feelings or emotions, and being unwilling to let go.

The ninth is attachment: pursuing desires and seeking more and more.

The tenth is being: possessing or existing; this kind of possessing or existing is empty and illusory and impermanent, and corresponds to the beginning of the operation of (causal conditions) coming together.

The eleventh is birth: empty, illusory, impermanent appearance, birth, production.

The twelfth is old age and death: the changes that happen to things and events and apparent forms, when the causal conditions that created them dissolve and scatter.

It is said: "Ignorance conditions action, action conditions consciousness, consciousness conditions name and form, name and form condition the six sense organs, the six sense organs condition contact, contact conditions sensation, sensation conditions craving, craving conditions attachment, attachment conditions being, being conditions birth, and birth conditions old age and death." This means that our ignorance brings about all sorts of actions, words, and states of consciousness, and these things form our understanding of the whole world. After a long time, this understanding becomes set concepts and biased perceptions. When you contact the world through the eyes, ears, nose, tongue, body, and conceptual mind, you will be under the influence of set concepts and biased perceptions, and you will generate biased perceptions of the world. Your biased perceptions will influence the feelings you get when you come in contact with things and events. When you crave these feelings, you want to hold onto them, and you even want to get more of them. So then, you will be impelled by desires to make choices that bring along the biased perceptions, and these choices will produce a result.

But at the same time this result is produced, it also implies that it will change, following changes in the foregoing causal elements.

This process is like a cotton thread soaked in gasoline: once you light the end of the "cotton thread," that is, use wisdom to see through ignorance, the flame will keep on spreading, and incinerate the whole thread till there is nothing left. At this point, your mind will be set free from the endless cycling. As it is said: "When ignorance is extinguished, action is extinguished; when action is extinguished, consciousness is extinguished, when consciousness is extinguished, name and form are extinguished; when name and form are extinguished, the six sense organs are extinguished: when the six sense organs are extinguished, contact is extinguished; when contact is extinguished, sensation is extinguished: when sensation is extinguished, craving is extinguished; when craving is extinguished, attachment is extinguished; when attachment is extinguished, being is extinguished; when being is extinguished, birth is extinguished; when birth is extinguished, old age and death are extinguished."

Life Is a Giant Dream

Most people are used to forgetting about the existence of "change." They can never discover that the whole world is like a dream, full of change. We always think that this scene that changes so often is permanent, and so when we get things, we are delighted, and when we lose things, we are full of sorrow, and when we face the unknown, we are fraught with anxieties. When we understand clearly that everything is like a dream or an illusion, will we still have all these cares?

Life is like a train with no beginning and no end. You can't remember when you go on the train, and all you know is that you wear some kind of clothes, and that some people chat with you, and some people rub shoulders with you as they pass by. You know that you have gone through some kind of story on the way, but it is hard to keep remembering it. Suddenly, at a certain time you are tired out, and then death appears. In just an instant, everything seems to start all over again from the beginning. But you could not recall that this is a new beginning. You completely forget another road you passed along before, other clothes you wore before, other people you met, you remembered, you forgot, other events you had encountered and forgotten. You just take this as the one and only beginning.

The cycle of birth and death has artistic beauty from the Buddhist point of view, but the real cycling just has pain. But does the cycling really exist? Perhaps it is only an image, perhaps it really exists. What we can say for sure is that everyone of us is continuously experiencing the cycle every day. In moments of relaxation and happiness, we are heavenly beings. In moments of hatred and anger, we are asuras, jealous spirits. In moments of stupidity and ignorance, we are animals. In moments of unbearable pain, we are in hell. In moments when we are full of desires and hopes, we are hungry ghosts. When we are tangled up in the travail of desire and conscience, we are human beings.

Is the basic cause that gives rise to this emotional cycling "causal conditions?" We can talk this way, but it is more tied to our bad memory. Most people are accustomed to forgetting about the existence of "change." They can never discover that the whole world is like a dream, full of change. We always think that this scene that changes so often is permanent, and so when we get things, we are delighted, and when we lose things, we are full of sorrow, and when we face the unknown, we are fraught with anxieties. When we understand clearly that everything is like a dream or an illusion, will we still have all these cares?

You close your eyes and recall many dreams from the past and imagine you are still in the dreams: those beautiful or frightening or sadly moving or absurd dreams. Isn't this like a movie that lets you savor it again and again? But why don't you crave the beauty of dreams, why aren't you saddened by the moving sadness of dreams, why aren't you frightened by the fearfulness of dreams? Because you clearly understand that what is gained and lost in dreams does not really exist. If you can take a step further and clearly understand that apparent reality is also a dream that mistakes the fake for the real, then you will be able to live life very independently.

I have cultivated "the method of achieving enlightenment by observing everything as a dream." This method is very interesting and effective. After cultivating it, you will slowly take hold of the power to control dreams. The feeling of controlling your dreams is very beautiful, because you are both the protagonist and the actor; since you are both a participant and a spectator, you will thereby experience the happiness of controlling the mind and spirit. When you have experienced this kind of happiness, you will discover that all the happy feelings brought to you by the external world cannot compare with the independence and freedom of the mind and spirit.

Let's take an example. In a dream you might encounter a person you have a crush on and to whom you offer all your love and sincerity unreservedly. Because you clearly know that this is a dream, no matter whether you lose or you gain, it all exists as an empty illusion, no different from a movie. All you can do is wholeheartedly play the role, and you do not have to worry about the results of your love. This way you can wholeheartedly enjoy the process of love, and the smiles and tears all become the same kind of poetic feeling and romance. In the dream, you may meet a terrifying wild beast whose fangs bite off your hand. You might be timid, but ultimately you are not afraid of the beast, because you know that in a dream, life and death are just false appearances. You may run away, or you may look for a weapon and an opportunity to counterattack. You pick up a sharp spear, and then the instant the beast goes to snap at you, you accurately and quickly pierce his skull with the spear, and your heart beats with a sense of success...

Not calculating the results—this is the advantage of dreams. Maybe in this dream that most people consider real, we will not meet wild beasts, and we will not fly into the sky, but we definitely can act as if we are in a dream, and look upon gain and loss as unimportant. How can we look upon them as unimportant? By going along with causal conditions, and not getting hung up on things that are not important—this is letting go of everything.

When some men and women are in love, as soon as they hear their partner speak of "letting go of everything," they feel frightened. This is because they are assessing things by the standard of whether or not their partner values them, and they often look at whether their partner is generating strong emotions toward them. Isn't this right? Actually, it is not right. Whether they are generating strong emotions toward you just shows that you can arouse their desires, like emotional desire, like possessive desire, like the desire to control, and so on. Genuine love is something grander. If a person genuinely loves you, that person will honor you and value you as he or she would honor and value his or her own life. The person will ignore his or her own feelings, and even sacrifice himself or herself, for the sake of making you blessed and happy. Genuine love is a kind of selflessness: it is very similar to the religious spirit.

Unfortunately, some people always cling to a good feeling between a man and a woman, and are constantly scheming to hold onto it. When they cannot possess their partners, they do not hesitate to destroy them, and are unwilling to let someone else possess them. For example, a student once told me that someone in her class liked a girl in the same class, but after revealing his feelings to her and being rejected, one day he assaulted that girl, and killed her, and buried her corpse on the top floor of a high-rise building. The student who told me the story asked, was this love? I told her, this is absolutely not love! There is absolutely no kind of love in the world that would let people harm others. This kind of so-called "love" is just a kind of desire that at first glance resembles the emotion of love. Many people take emotional desire as love, and that is why so many murderers act in the name of "love." This is because many people, when they can love, do not understand love, and when they are finally able to understand love, they have often lost the opportunity for love. This is why only after seeing through the red dusts of the sensory world, can some people take the love they have built on a certain person and transform it into a greater love that takes all living beings as its object, a kind of religious spirit that is very similar to love.

There are many misunderstandings like this in human life. This is why Buddhists think that the reason why humans suffer, if we trace it back to its root, is because of ignorance. Because they are ignorant, they mistake the false for the true, and cling to illusion as reality. We take things that are clearly empty and illusory and impermanent, and view them as real, and then when they dissolve away and perish, we feel pain and suffering. This is like clearly knowing in your mind that you cannot hold onto water, but being unwilling to face this, and instead always trying to hold onto it. What real meaning is there in that? When you clearly understand that even life is all a great illusion, you will stop caring so much about everything.

We think that birth is the beginning of life, and death is the end of life, but this is not the true characteristic of life. Causal conditions are constantly flowing along and transforming, and life too is constantly flowing along and transforming. You have surely seen children at the beach building sandcastles—do they have a solid immutable inherent nature? They are sand, they are castles — are they both that, or are they both not that? In reality, a sandcastle is an apparent form made by its elements coming together, and when the causal conditions dissolve, and new causal conditions are added — like the ocean wind and the encroachment of waves — it then changes into something else, it does not have an unchanging inherent nature. Humans are like this too; all apparent phenomena in the world are all like this, including birth and death. Birth and death imply switching states, they imply that the distinction is even clearer, that the change is even easier for the physical eye and the consciousness to grasp. The change does not only take place at the instant of birth or death. It is like an apartment building depreciating: people are constantly in the process of aging. There are more subtle changes going on all the time, like cellular replacement and the constant change of thinking patterns and so on.

When you have understood this point, you will understand that in fact life is just a giant dream.

The "Self" Is a Giant Illusion

From inside to outside, there is no way we can find an unchanging "me." Since there is no unchanging "me," how could there be "my" family, "my" house, "my" car, and all the rest of it?

We have said that the true characteristic of life is that it is a giant dream. So then, what about people? What is the true characteristic of "people?"

The true characteristic of "people" is also that they are an illusion, a kind of play of elements coming together, like children building with blocks. At a certain moment, the children use the blocks to build a little castle. This "castle" is something that exists within a certain period of time, and the children will soon knock it down, and build something else. So we say that the existence of the "castle" is an illusion. When the elements that are put together to form it come apart, it will crumble. Human life and the human body are also this way. Our ways of thinking, our emotions, our health, our internal physical environment, our outward appearance, our course in life—all these will change every minute following the ceaselessly changing flow of causal conditions. There is no fixed, unchanging situation; no independent essence that does not pass through birth and go toward death. Thus, speaking from the level of ultimate meaning, there is no "castle built of blocks" that really exists, and there is no "person" that truly exists. Everything is covered with a term to show the subtle distinctions, the "apparent forms" that are really the same as the real basic substance. If we say that there is some great distinction between ourselves and the building made of wooden blocks, it is that we have a "soul" — what I mean is not a soul as in "spiritual self" — which we are equipped with and with which we can recognize the true mind, and fully awaken to the true characteristic of life.

If your mind and spirit are covered by desires, then you will have no way to recognize the true self, and no way to fully awaken to the true characteristic of life. You may think that in the world a "self" genuinely exists, and it continuously possesses things and loses things. In reality, this so-called "self" is no more than another thing that arises from the coming together of causal conditions. Our physical bodies are not inherent: their birth, health, and growth require that they depend on many external conditions, like the union of the father and mother, good food, ample nutrition, a secure environment to grow up in, and so on. Moreover, the cells in our bodies are constantly being born and dying off, and our vital functions and our external appearances are constantly changing. Our intellects, our viewpoints, our habits, our standards of conduct are very individual, but none of them are inherent; they too are things resulting from the coming together of causal conditions, and they are constantly undergoing changes due to external factors. So then, from internal to external, there is no way we can find any unchanging "self." Since there is no unchanging "self," how could there be "my" family, "my" house, "my" car, and all the rest of it?

Speaking at the level of basic substance, the whole world is like this. It is equivalent to us, there is no distinction at all. For this reason, there exists no opposition of standpoint or viewpoint. The afflictions of many people lie in their not understanding this point. They either put themselves in opposition to the world, or make a distinction between "you" and "me," and they waste a lot of brain power and time calculating and comparing, and produce many forms of clinging and attachment. Thus, people who are in favorable circumstances busy themselves with seeking higher desires, and those who are in adverse circumstances busy themselves with anger and resentment, and even take vengeance on an external world that cannot satisfy their desires.

What is the so-called external world? In reality, it is the projection of various kinds of apparent forms in our inner minds. When we still have not yet been enlightened, all we can do is interpret the world assuming we are right, but this kind of interpretation cannot represent the true characteristic of the world. For example, when you hear someone rebuking you, you feel that you have suffered an insult, and so you feel very angry. But in fact, both the sense of being insulted and the anger are products of your ears and your mind functioning together. If you had not heard them, or you did not care about them, could someone else's insults hurt your feelings? This is why we say that what punishes you is your own mind.

In my writings, I often express my own point of view forthrightly, so it is impossible to make everyone like me. Sometimes friends tell me that someone is insulting me again, and I always laugh it off. On the other hand, when friends praise me highly, I will write something along the lines of "Xuemo is a donkey" to express myself. Why is this? It is because I know that this world is illusory transformation, and everything is memory. As causal conditions flow and change, the people who criticized you may become your most loyal friends, and the people who praised you may cook up all kinds of schemes to bury you. Nothing in the world is fixed and immutable. Therefore I do not concern myself with it, and I do not have time to care about it. All I can do is value and hold precious the time when I am alive, and use appropriate methods to do things that benefit the world. As for whether or not the world will accept me, or welcome me, that is the world's business — it will be enough if I have done my part properly.

Oftentimes, if we think about all the changes in life, we will look upon individual gain and loss more indifferently. In the end, the bodies that accompany us through our lives are not permanent things.

At the outset we are just a fertilized ovum; when certain conditions come together, we develop and take shape, and then we are born. From being a baby the size of a kitten, we grow up and mature into adults who can live independently, take on responsibilities, and form families. The changes involved in this cannot be called minor. But at the same time we happily accept these interesting changes, we also must accept those changes that are not so interesting, like the aging of the body, and the decline of physical strength, and the erosion of beauty, and so on. This is because in basic substance our bodies are like houses and furniture—they are all things formed by the coming together of causal conditions, and it is impossible for them to avoid undergoing changes, as the old causal conditions dissolve and new causal conditions come together.

The contradiction is that when we are crazy about making money, smoking, drinking alcohol, indulging in mad revelry, we are totally unaware that we are creating the conditions that promote aging, and even more unaware that this will reduce our lifespans. We always feel that we will be able to live for several more decades, but who knows? This is why I say, the physical body is a big lie, and beauty based on the physical body is an even bigger lie. It is a false form that can ingratiate itself with other people and with ourselves, and can induce desires and anger and strife.

There is a movie that describes a funny yet also sad story: ten years of war, dead bodies everywhere were caused by men's desire to take the beauty of women as their own. What an absurd state of affairs! But there are many events like this in history — ancient and modern, here and abroad. Why is this? It is because desire and false thoughts cover people's eyes, and make people unable to see the true characteristic of the world clearly.

After you see the light of the real characteristic, and this dissolves away the many desires and false thoughts, you will discover that many of the world's concepts are no more than concepts, that they are labels created by people. The true characteristic is much simpler than the concepts. When you clearly understand this point, you will discover that all gains and losses are just a dream. You will also discover that you have been patronizing a dream, and on the other hand, forgetting to do all those things that have real meaning and genuine constructive value. Sometimes it may even become a regret that you cannot remedy in this lifetime.

What Do People Live For?

Late at night when everyone is quiet and you cannot sleep, have you ever asked your mind and spirit this kind of question: "What do people live for?" Birth, old age, sickness, death, being separated from those you love, being put together with those you hate, being unable to find the answer, the five poisons of greed, anger, ignorance, arrogance and doubt blazing up. Human life has so much suffering, and the only refuge is death. Even the planet earth cannot avoid facing destruction one day. So then, why do people have to go through all this, and go on living in such pain?

People always ask me: Is our fate in life created by karma or not? Is our fate in life already a fixed constant? I tell them that a "fixed constant" is the program of a mind that is already dead. People who are alive can create their causal conditions. When the mind changes, then fate changes. If you do good deeds and create good karma, you will obtain good results. If you do bad deeds and create bad karma, you will obtain bad results. All choices, behavior, and outcomes do not lie outside of the mind, so I always say: "Great virtue shapes the mind, and fate in life is created by mind."

In the diverse human crowd, with all kinds of shapes and colors, you will see two kinds of fate. Selfish people see their own gain and loss as important, and in all their actions, they are sure to make protecting their own gains their top priority. This implies that they may tell lies, or even do things that injure others to benefit themselves. Their actions are sure to bring about aversion and defensiveness from other people. Unselfish people value things in themselves, and all they do is for the sake of doing things well, to serve other people. So even if they do not have enough capacity, and cannot do things perfectly, they are sure to win other people's trust. If they constantly strengthen their own capacity, naturally they will be able to gain even more opportunities to serve.

I grew up in a farming village, without any special background, and without any strong economic support. I went through many things the world would see as rough patches and reverses, and even things that could be reckoned as bad luck, but these experiences were never able to shake my dream and my quest, but on the contrary, they all became steps to realizing my dream. Why was this? It was because I transformed them into nutrition for living, and with their nourishment my mind and spirit grew stronger day by day. Moreover, although I was lazy about managing my connections with people, and lazy about doing the things that intelligent people never get bored with, many kind people still appeared in my life, and they unselfishly provided me with a lot of help, and created many precious opportunities for me. For this, I am very grateful to them. At the same time, I also understand that if I had been a selfish, arrogant person who made no attempts to make progress, these opportunities would have gone to those people who were more worthy of having them than I.

Because of this, I always say to students that there is no failure, there is only giving up. I did not have natural talent, and I was not hardworking. I just faced in a certain direction, and every day I traveled the road I had to travel, without stopping, without wandering off, without being deceived, and finally I woke up. Sometimes there would be a girl who beckoned to me, and I could exchange a few words with her, but I did not forget the goal of my quest and run off after her. This was because I clearly knew that she would lead me toward another road. When money beckoned me, I also would not go. I always affirmed my own direction. Let's not talk about me: even an ant who crawls every day for ten years will have covered a very long way. Success is this simple. The only thing to fear is giving up, because that represents the mind's wavering. Once the mind wavers, all the persistence will lose its meaning, and all the obstructions will appear with a strength they never had before, and you will unconsciously make many choices that are totally at odds with the choices you made before. You also might utterly lose your direction, and waste your life away. When you reach old age, you might be leaning on a handrail by the riverside, blankly staring into the distance, and giving a sigh. Then you will say to your son: "Your dad passed his life in a daze, and now I have reached this age, achieving nothing and having no dreams." In the end, several decades of time are summed up in a single sentence, and then what meaning will all the ups and downs in your life have had?

Once there was a reporter who visited a shepherd boy. The reporter asked, "Why do you herd sheep?" The shepherd boy said, "To make money." The reporter asked, "What do you want to do with the money you've made?" The shepherd boy said, "Marry a wife, and raise children and have grandchildren." The reporter also asked, "In the future, what do you plan to have your grandchildren do?" The shepherd boy replied, "Herd sheep." These days many people are like this. They study hard in order to find a good job in the future, they find a good job in order to make money, buy a house, get married to a pretty wife. They marry a pretty wife in order to have children and bring them up well, and when the children grow up, they make them study hard so they can find a good job... Isn't this kind of life track going in a cycle? When you talk like this, aren't you aware that no matter how "splendid" a life you lead, you are doing no more than copying the pattern of other people's lives, a pattern of life that will not leave any traces, or create any value?

Of course, this kind of life also has its advantages, and can satisfy this kind of person, and can yield some petty pleasures. But are you really willing to live this way just to greet your future death? Search your conscience. Late at night when everyone is quiet and you cannot sleep, have you ever asked your mind and spirit this kind of question: "What do people live for?" Birth, old age, sickness, death, being separated from those you love, being put together with those you hate, being unable to find the answer, the five poisons of greed, anger, ignorance, arrogance and doubt blazing up. Human life has so much suffering, and the only refuge is death. Even the planet earth cannot avoid facing destruction one day. So then, why do people have to go through all this, and go on living in such pain? Does it make any difference how long you live? Why can't you close your eyes and simply meet death then and there? I believe that many people who choose suicide decide to end their own lives because they cannot answer this question. If they knew that life has countless possibilities, maybe they would not choose to abandon it. But when they have lost their physical bodies, will they have attained the liberation they wanted?

Being alive is always better than being dead, because only when you are alive can you remedy the many regrets of this lifetime, and correct the many mistakes in your life. But the prerequisite for everything is that you must have a mind and spirit that are strong and filled with wisdom.

This is because your perception of the world is the manifestation of your mind and spirit, and all your actions are also manifestations of your mind and spirit. Take a company for example: you are aware that it is filled with intrigue and struggles for gain, that it is a fiery pit, but other people consider it full of opportunity and challenges, and think that it is a fine place for training the body and mind. Take another example: your home has ninety square meters, but you still think it is too small. But when friends visit, they exclaim, "My home is half the size of yours!" If you understand this point, then you understand that everything is like dewdrops in the sunlight, like last night's dreams: very soon it disappears, so there cannot be much more to calculate. Only when you do not calculate so many things, will you discover that this world is full of nourishment waiting for you to absorb, that this world is a giant treasure house.

Why do we care about so many things? Because we think our bodies are "selves," we focus on their feelings, and in the midst of so many desires, we get deluded and lose track of our own direction. But we forget that this physical body is easily destroyed, that it is an illusory transformation. No matter how we try to cling to it, it will always be destroyed. So then, while our bodies exist, we must do things that benefit living beings. Your actions make up the value of your human life. You must realize that the existence of your physical body is like an insect flying through space, and cannot leave any traces. But the spirit upheld in your actions will detach from the fetters of your physical body and be propagated on, and become a beneficial nourishment for humankind. After we understand this point, before our physical bodies dissolve away, we must establish an enduring merit helping sentient beings, in order to realize the highest value of human life.

Section Two:

Discover the Inherent Treasure of Life

The treasury of Life, Every One Possesses

You have to use your mind and spirit to feel the world,
use your mind and spirit to feel life, use your mind and spirit
to feel the inherent body of life. You must have a dialog with
your own mind and spirit, and you must deduce the most
simple truth from all the various apparent forms being born
and being extinguished, just like the Buddha's experience
under the bodhi tree. Only when you do this, will you be able
to discover the inherent treasure of life.

In my novel *The Spells of Xixia*, the protagonist Khyung is a
very significant figure. What I was pointing out was that Khyung,
who was an ascetic monk on a pilgrimage, was really also the
guardian spirit in *Desert Rites* who went to another village seeking
his dream. He traveled very far, and broadened his knowledge by
seeing many people and events, but he was not able to find the so-
called holy land. Later he returned to the run-down Vajra house,
and there he saw the seed mantra of the Vajra Yogini (one of the
spirit totems of those who cultivate practice). At this point he
understood that the place he had been seeking all along was his

own home village.

For many years, I was traveling on a "pilgrimage," and I did not care what temples I passed through. One year I visited almost all the temples on Mount Wutai, but I did not remember the name of a single one. All I could remember was that in the space of many months, I peacefully traveled that "pilgrimage" route. In my mind the pilgrimage was not going to see some temple buildings or physical scenery, but was purely a matter of a yearning and a reverence for a kind of spirit. All my pilgrimages were just to cleanse my own spirit, and make myself merge into one great energy and dissolve away "self-clinging."

It is not difficult to understand the meaning of the words of this statement in theory, but if you want to genuinely understand it, you must look within, and focus on your own mind and spirit, and forget about everything the external world puts on you, including various forms of common sense, theory, knowledge, experience, and even your physical body. You have to use your mind and spirit to feel the world, use your mind and spirit to feel life, use your mind and spirit to feel the inherent body of life. You must have a dialog with your own mind and spirit, and you must deduce the most simple truth from all the various apparent forms being born and being extinguished, just like the Buddha's experience under the bodhi tree. Only when you do this, will you be able to discover the inherent treasure of life, and gain the wisdom of liberation.

Perhaps we should not say "gain," because this wisdom

does not depend on someone else bestowing it, nor is it a kind of discovery, nor is it something that exists apart from you — it is something that is inherently there. So let's change how we describe it, and use the word "open" (rather than "gain"): open the treasury of wisdom in your life, open the spiritual flower garden of your inner mind, open the secret code of happiness that is within you. We can also say "discover:" discover your inherent happiness, discover your inherent light of wisdom. People who cultivate practice work hard for years, but this is just to sweep the mind clean of the dirt that has accumulated over the years, and break the hard shell enclosing the mind and spirit. This lets their own minds become soft and supple, keen and sharp, and have a love that knows everything and tolerates everything but is not blind. This kind of love is founded on the basis of discovering inherent wisdom. The light of this inherent wisdom is the natural spontaneous wisdom of the inherent nature of mind. It is what Buddhists call "inherent original mind," and it is also called the true mind. The true mind accompanies the inherent nature of the minds of sentient beings all along; there is no gap, and it cannot be interrupted. It's just that many people cannot recognize it. When we recognize it, true mind appears. When we cannot recognize it, dark clouds block the sun, but we cannot say that then there is no sun. The sun exists all along; it's just that the clouds of false mind cover the sun.

True mind is like the sun. Although it does not have the

warmth of the sun, still, it can illuminate the dark night of a person's mind and spirit, and enable people to bid farewell to all delusion and confusion, and clearly see the true characteristic of life, and find the direction for human life and the meaning of living. It is like opening a curtain and letting the bright sunshine enter into a dark room. The instant you illuminate mind and see its inherent nature, everything becomes pure and bright. Illuminating mind and seeing its inherent nature — this is enlightenment, this is recognizing true mind and seeing empty inherent nature.

When your mind and spirit become empty, pure, clear and bright, you will be absolutely unwilling to use thoughts to disturb it. You will savor it as if savoring a cup of fine pure tea. All the things which once made you pursue things like a hungry wolf pursuing its prey then all become dull and insipid, and you will not understand what you would endure so much pain and suffering for, why you pursued them oblivious of everything, but you won't feel like thinking about the reasons anymore. You pursued them, okay, and then you gave them up, okay: whether you went wrong, or got it right, okay — it's all gone. All you want is to savor this tranquility, to cherish all you have before your eyes, and to concentrate on each moment. This is because you clearly understand that all you can control is the present moment. Everything becomes simple and natural. Everything is like flowing water, continuously moving forward. Your thinking, your mind, will never again be imprisoned somewhere in the past. You will finally understand what is meant by "living in the here and now." One of my students said to me that before, she had always felt that the territory of her life was very large, large enough to surround her: that was her world. But when she rode in an airplane, and she looked down and saw the lands and buildings looking so small, she discovered that the world was much bigger than she had imagined it. It included not only the city where she lived and the people around her, but also the whole universe, and countless living things. In fact, it is like this. Human beings are not the masters of the world and of the universe. All that one person can control is his or her own mind and spirit. One day you may truly become the master of your mind and spirit, and then the world in your mind will be totally transformed, and your feelings toward the world will be entirely different.

The true mind is something inherent in life, but not every person is able to recognize it. For people who are fully equipped with genuine faith, recognizing the true mind is as easy as turning over their hand. For people who do not have the mind of faith, recognizing the true mind is as difficult as touching the sky. The most difficult part lies in its quality of "don't speak, don't speak — once you speak, you go wrong." It is like love: only those who have genuinely been in love know what kind of feeling love is. When you stop all miscellaneous thoughts, and observe your own inherent mind, you will discover that you mind is fundamentally a transparent crystal. This is a realm that cannot be described with something as pale and feeble as language. This is because, for people who have never tasted the finest Longjing tea, no description of Longjing tea can enable them to understand its flavor. This is why all I can do is guide you to discover the treasury of your inner mind — you yourself must make this journey of seeking it.

You may not like making this journey. You might feel as if you are traveling through an endless dark night, getting your fill of the torments of not knowing and being confused, not knowing whether the direction you are going is correct or not, and not knowing when you will finally be able to get to the end of the dark night. You might not even know whether or not this dark night has an end. It might seem that in your world there is no daylight. In the dark night, you stumble along in one direction that may be correct, with the mud and gravel chafing your body, getting your body soaked in the muddy water from under the ground. You get very fatigued, but you do not want to give up: you go forward resolutely in your great yearning. You know that coming out of the dark night is the most important thing in your life. In this resolute certainty, there will suddenly appear a feeble bit of light, and in that instant, all your thoughts will dissolve away, and all that will be in your mind will be purity and joy. Your footsteps will finally have direction, and your mind will be filled with strength. You will be able to hear your heart beating strong and solid, and you will feel no more fear. You will have direction, and your mind will be filled with strength, and you may even be able to feel your strong heartbeat. You will know how to eliminate the damage caused by all barriers and defilements, and you will feel that this cannot be counted as damage. It's like this: you know that the person you deeply love is beyond a forest of thorns, and to see her, you are willing to endure the pain of the thorns pricking you all over. That pain will all dissolve away, and everything that has happened will all become proof of the journey you made for love. During that painful struggle, your love and your mind and spirit, which had been fragile and weak, have become stronger day by day, and in the end you cannot be bothered by external things. This process is truly filled with a moving poetic quality.

True Happiness Is a Light in the Mind

True happiness is in fact very simple: it is the light in your mind. Perhaps you feel this to be inconceivable, but things are always this simple, aren't they? Those most beautiful tulips in the world, which you traveled all over the world looking for, are actually in full bloom in your own garden. Too bad if you never discovered them.

Apart from "love," the word that is the easiest for people in the world to misunderstand is probably "happiness." Many people who think they understand happiness in fact do not understand what true happiness is. They generally take the feeling that is produced when desires are satisfied to be true happiness. For example, they generally think that the more a person has, the happier that person will be, and the more famous a person is, the happier that person will be. Simply put, happiness in their view must be based on certain material conditions. Obviously this kind of happiness is unreliable.

This is because, to develop the conditions that foster "happiness," many people inevitably exhaust themselves seeking external things. Among these people, some are constantly gaining, and some are constantly losing, and some are still seeking without results, but none of them can find true happiness. With those who are constantly gaining, what they gain are not the things they really want, but rather some impermanent external things and even more impermanent happy feelings. Thus, what comes in quick succession is inevitably the loss created when expectation and reality do not match. People who are constantly losing think that if only they would get something, then they would be able to achieve happiness, but they still cannot get things to go as they wish, and so they fall into a great sense of loss. People who pursue things without any results, while in the process of pursuing them, even forget what ultimately they are looking for. All they can do is follow their own footsteps from yesterday, and keep on going ahead blindly step by step, getting farther and farther away from true happiness...

So then, in the end, what is true happiness? Before I answer this question of yours, probably you must first make a slight adjustment to your state of mind. Otherwise, you may not be able to understand what I say. Look and see. If I say to you that true happiness is just a feeling of the mind and spirit, will you be able to understand the full meaning of this statement? Will you be able to experience this kind of purity of the spirit? Maybe not. This is because this is a value you may not have thoroughly understood, or you may never have experienced. It is like me: it comes from that deep yellow earth of the Western Regions. It is absolutely different from that attitude of materialistic pride and bias of contemporary people. So please first try to completely forget about those ideal models related to apartment buildings and cars and salaries and stock shares and even wives and children and all such things, and at least for a short time screen them out. Only when you do this, can you let down your defenses, and enter into the "world" I am going to describe.

I always say, I do not want to change the world: what I want to change is just myself. I do not want to illuminate the world: what I want to illuminate is just myself. I do not want to use literature to make the whole world listen to me, and I do not want to use my writings to broadcast anything. I am just having a chat with the literary world. All the goals of my cultivating practice are to let myself achieve absolute independence and happiness, that's all.

As luck would have it, there are many people in this world who have the same needs as me — they too are seeking this kind of independence and happiness. Ultimately, seeking love and freedom is basically the inherent nature of humans. Since I realized this before them, I must take the road I have traveled and offer it to them. For this reason, in all my written works, I say things which many people may not be able to understand, and which they may not have the patience to listen to, but these are all the words in my mind. I believe that after they read these words, those people who are on the same frequency as I will all be able to smile. Perhaps these words will only be able to bring these friends a good state of mind, or a bit of awakening, and this too is good. Some friends and students have also told me that these words, which my true mind has revealed, have even helped them restore their courage for living, their dreams and their love, and the strength to transform their ordinary lives. This is very good. However, for me, this is definitely not an unexpected thing, because I too have traveled on a journey like this.

Although I have looked this way all along — having a beard, wearing a robe with long red sleeves, wearing pale blue loose-fitting trousers, being unconcerned and happy, always free and at ease, as if nobody is around — I have also gone through a journey of spiritual searching. On this point, I am no different from all those children seeking happiness and not being able to find it. Thus, I really understand them, and perhaps I also really understand you.

You keep your head down and travel your night road, sometimes thinking about the past, sometimes hoping for the future. You cannot discern the existence of the bright moon. Especially when you go into the shade of a forest or of the high-rise buildings, you have a stronger feeling that you have been swallowed up by the infinite darkness. All around you are flickering secretive shadows, and so your mind is filled with loneliness, desolation, and fear. But once you put a stop to your endless thoughts, and lift up your head, and gaze into the depths of the night sky, then you discover, not knowing where it started, that in this backdrop of night, ultimately there is a clear bright moon accompanying you. It is tranquil and silent, but it is as if a warm laugh has come forth from the silence, and this laughter soaks into your mind, and stirs up a feeling like a wave of warm water, and surprisingly you become aware of the beauty and wonder of the night where everything is silent. And from this, you change, as you trudge through the darkness of night, and you are no longer alone, and the bright moon's laughter fills your mind and spirit, and changes the journey into something exceptionally poetic.

I wrote a bit of doggerel: the purpose was to dispel the way some people were "deifying" me, and it also expressed my mind: "Xuemo is a donkey, traveling the road with his head down. When he happens to lift his head, he sees the moon in the sky. Seeking wisdom without wisdom, seeking knowledge without knowledge. It's just that the mind has light, and because of this he is not sad." This is right. An enlightened me is that donkey with a light in his mind.

True happiness is in fact very simple: it is the light in your mind. Perhaps you feel this to be inconceivable, but things are always this simple, aren't they? Those most beautiful tulips in the world, which you traveled all over the world looking for, are actually in full bloom in your own garden. Too bad if you never discovered them. When you are the way I was in the past, when you "happen to lift your head," you will see that pure, still, poetic moonlight in your mind. Then you will slowly come out of that long dark night, and from then on, you will not be sad.

All Are Memories, Past and Gone

If you establish happiness on something that is formed by the coming together of causal conditions, this implies that your happiness will be conditional. Once that thing your happiness depends on dissolves away with the scattering of those causes and conditions, your happiness too will dissolve away. Happiness that is based on external things will not last, no matter what the external things are.

Maybe some friends will ask: "Ultimately, how much happiness is true happiness? How does true happiness differ from happy feelings?" There is no way for me to take this feeling and fill your mind with it, but I can tell you this: if you recognize true mind, then you will discover that all happiness you get by depending on external objects cannot compare to the inherent "heaven" of your inner mind. This is because everything in the external world is always continuously changing.

For example, you scrimp and save in order to buy a new cellphone, but it soon malfunctions, so what then? You may immediately start thinking of an even newer model of cellphone. Take another example. You hope that by buying a BMW you will make your clients notice you more, but when you buy the BMW, you discover instead that people do not care what car you drive, they have begun to care about other things. What should you do then?

If you establish happiness on something that is formed by the coming together of causal conditions, this implies that your happiness will be conditional. Once that thing your happiness depends on dissolves away with the scattering of those causes and conditions, your happiness too will dissolve away. Happiness that is based on external things will not last, no matter what the external things are. Then too, this kind of happiness is just a kind of feeling, and feeling is a kind of memory, and memories are things that will be lost. So then, this hope of making yourself happy through external things is without a doubt a great contradiction. With this kind of expectation, you will constantly experience the pain of loss. Even if you get what you want, you will feel worries about gain and loss, and you will have no way of enjoying the happiness you have. Obviously then, happiness founded on external things is something that will not last, no matter what these external things are. After you clearly understand this point, when you re-examine the many things you have very much cared about, you will discover that in reality they have no meaning. Nothing in the world has any true meaning, because nothing will last forever. There is no fundamental distinction between having them and losing them, and so none of them are worth caring about. But this does not imply that a person should be concerned with anything, and drift along at random. On the contrary, understanding the natural law of causal origination and causal extinction is to let you have a more positive, active life.

I'll give a simple example. If you know your beloved is suffering from a terminal illness, and she has just a month left to live, you will love her dearly, as you would love a rare treasure, and cherish and enjoy every minute and every second you spend with her. You feel that as long as she is still alive, you are already very fortunate. At a time like this, you will not care whether or not she treats you well, whether or not she does every detail of life well, whether or not she can be perfect in your eyes etc. By the same principle, only when you recognize that all things are continuously changing, will you put aside all calculations, and truly live in the present moment.

But this is still an inference, and inferences bear the marks of thinking. Thinking is thought: it is another kind of memory. But true mind is not logic, not the result of inference. It is the most inherently real thing, the wisdom fundamentally inherent in life. It is not elusive and erratic, changing a thousand times every instant. It does not change along with external objects: since it has no empty illusory birth, it has no empty illusory extinction. But in the same way, it is not vacuous and empty, with nothing there. When there is nothing there, when it's dead and still, it is inert emptiness, not the true mind. Only that which can give rise to wondrous functioning is the true mind. The wondrous functioning of the true mind is being alive in the present moment, clearly understanding the present moment, being enlightened in the present moment. That also means every minute that you must abide in peace in the true mind, abide in peace in the empty inherent nature, maintain lucid awareness, uphold correct mindfulness. You must not let desires control your mind, and you must not sink into oblivion so you do not respond to anything. It is like knowing you are thirsty, so you drink a cup of water, but you do not calculate whether this water is good or not, and you don't tie yourself up thinking about why you did not buy something else to drink—this is the wondrous functioning of the true mind. My writing is the wondrous functioning of the true mind, and when we serve sentient beings, this too is the wondrous functioning of the true mind. The wondrous functioning of the true mind is something that adapts to circumstances, and has no set form, and can extend to everything in the world. If, whatever you are doing, you are pure and lucid, you are your own master, and you are not controlled by selfish desires, then this is the true mind giving rise to wondrous functioning. This is because you clearly understand that everything in the world is memory—whatever you eat, whatever you drink, whoever you chat with, whatever other people tell you—all these are things that have passed you by. Whether you calculate and compare or not, you cannot really change anything, and there is nothing that does not pass you by. After you clearly understand this fact, you will not suffer loss, and you will not feel pain and suffering any more. You will discover that adapting to conditions is truly a good thing. If you can truly adapt to conditions, then no "issues" will exist in this world, and there will only be "apparent forms;" there will not be any "pain and suffering," only "experience" and "nourishment."

It's too bad that we are always being deluded by the world's false appearances. When we are deluded, we will feel that we have encountered a barrier we cannot cross, that there is no way for life to continue, we will see no hope, and our bodies and minds will be exhausted with fatigue. Sometimes our inner minds will still have another voice that takes advantage of the moment to speak to us and say: Why do you want to go on living? Living is too tiring — it would be better to die. When you are dead, everything will be resolved. You will no longer have to worry that people look down on you, that you don't have enough to eat, losing your means of living, that the people you love will abandon you... You will no longer have to worry about anything. So one day the stock market crashes and there is someone whose hopes are dashed and he jumps off a building and commits suicide. Who knew that as soon as he hit the ground, the stock market would bounce back? In his imagination, his family went bankrupt and his wife and children left, and he was out on the street without enough to eat, and other disasters struck. Actually, everything will be changing, and it was just his guesses that harmed him. This is the way the world is. Gigantic disasters are created by people's false minds.

When you have enough lucid awareness and knowledge of the truth, you will be able to leap out of the external circumstances where so many apparent forms objectify and evaluate you, and then you will discover that they are all filled with uncertainty. This implies that you certainly must take responsibility for the results produced by your own choices and actions. But these results are not necessarily as impossible to accept as you imagined, because the world is impermanent, and filled with all sorts of variables. As for that pitiful man (who committed suicide when the stock market crashed), his death was a variable, and stock prices rising again was a variable, and the dissolving away of the emotion of fear was also a variable. Furthermore, if he could have abided in peace in the true mind, and not been under the control of his desires, and he had lucidly evaluated this own ability to accept the situation, and had gone ahead and invested, then he would not have made this irrevocable choice, and he would not have thrown away his life after his investment was lost. If he had been able to abide in peace in the true mind, it is even possible that he would have taken the money he invested and used it to develop enterprises that served the public good or helped other people — this too would have been very good. This is another variable. When the mind changes, the world changes, and one's life is created by one's mind. It is a pity that he deliberately chose death. This is why what is lamentable for people is not a matter of the things they encounter, but that they use a wrong attitude to face human life.

While we are unable to choose our own fate, we are still able to choose our attitude toward life. It is just like what Laoshun always says in my novel *Desert Rites*: "What heaven can give, heaven's children can accept." Giving by heaven is a demonstration of heaven's mightiness while accepting by heaven's children is due to human dignity.

The interesting thing is, when you have a noble attitude, and calmly accept everything in your fate, including those things that the great majority of people are unwilling to accept, you will discover that actually the greatest thing is also no more than a memory. Be it the thing itself, or the feeling of pain and loss, they all ultimately pass away, and they cannot last forever.

Human Life Is a Continuous Struggle with "The Self"

The oceanic "true mind" is as even as the surface of a mirror, but when external objects are reflected in it, it is like the wind blowing and waves arising on the great ocean, and then false mind appears. When we use the power of wisdom or discipline to fend off the enticements of the external world and keep them outside the mind, the ocean of the mind slowly quiets down again. That state without waves or ripples is the true mind.

In my book *The Grey Wolf of Xixia*, I described a "woman" called White Robe. She was a ghost who had almost been dispelled. Why had she almost been dispelled? Because most people do not believe in the existence of spirits, and this kind of doubt was constantly dispelling her, until in the end, even she began to doubt herself. Later, Hei Geshou's appearance rescued her. This process in fact also occurs in the world of our inner minds. When we are slaves to desire, we constantly use a kind of utilitarian thinking to dispel our own spirits, and to dissolve away those yearnings of our inner minds to go toward the spiritual. We do not know that we can only realize a kind of relative eternity in those yearnings, but instead we keep on always seeking the eternal in the empty, illusory, impermanent external world. This kind of ignorance constantly dissolves away our power to find happiness; luckily the true mind is quietly waiting all along in that now hidden, apparent place in our minds. It has no beginning and no end; it is not born and not extinguished. It will not be dissolved away because we misunderstand it, and it will not be obliterated because we overlook it. In the *Diamond Sutra* it says: "They come from nowhere and go nowhere, so they are called the Tathagatas, the ones who come from reality." This Tathagata is the true mind.

Although the true mind is fundamentally inherent, many people are not able to recognize it. When you are not clear about the true mind, the false mind will drag you off, and you will become an ordinary person. But sometimes the true mind and the false mind will keep battling. When the true and the false attack each other, it will seem that you have become two people, and your personality will begin to split, and you and the other you will keep fighting.

In Western animated films they have taken this kind of "split personality" and given it form: they take the "true mind" personality and make it into an angel, and take the "false mind" personality and make it into a devil. When they receive a certain external stimulus, the confrontation between the angel and the devil breaks out in the world of the person's inner mind and cannot be resolved. This metaphor is very true to life. In Buddhism we often talk about "conquering the demons," but these demons are not in the form of humans or animals: they are the false thoughts that delude the human mind. False thoughts reflect human desires and biased perceptions, and represent an aspect of the animal nature of our inner minds. They are a kind of delusion that can use the false to confuse the real, and they are also a kind of blindfold. They do not want to let us see the real characteristic of things, and so they are constantly whispering in our ears, throwing our tranquility into confusion, and preventing us from listening to the voice of the true mind, especially when we are not clear about the true mind. What they point toward is usually the greedy desires of hungry ghosts, the anger and hatred of asuras, and the stupidity and ignorance of animals.

If you cannot clearly understand the true mind, and you blindly follow the direction of false thoughts, then there will be absolutely no way for you to reach that other shore of your dreams, and to reach absolute happiness and freedom. This is because, when you are tangled up in false thoughts, you always take those false thoughts as "the other" and your own mind as "myself." Then a strong dualism will appear in your mind, and in this dualism, you will make a clear division between yourself and the external world, and no matter what you do, you will always have to separate "you" and "I." I lose something, you gain something.

Originally it should belong to me, but you took it away. I gave so much, but you did not give me anything in return... These things are all fundamentally empty illusory memories, no matter whether you gained or you lost; they are all impermanent apparent forms, and in basic substance they are one thing. But when you are lost in confusion due to false thoughts, you will mistake the false for the true, and take illusory perception as true reality, and do all kinds of stupid things, and these actions will bring on the corresponding karmic force. If you build a good causal basis, you go up, and if you build an evil causal basis, you go down—thus you revolve in the six planes of existence. But even then, the true mind is still unmoved and unshaken. It is like a pine tree rooted in bedrock: though the branches may shake, the trunk is still firmly rooted. When you abide in peace in the true mind, you understand that all things are dreams, illusions, bubbles, undergoing myriad changes every instant, not worth being concerned with—then illusory forms melt away like dewdrops in the blazing sun.

Thus we say that illusory thoughts are very much to be feared. They can take you far away from love and wisdom, and make you cling to empty illusory individual gain and loss, and make simple things complicated. They can also make you sink into inexplicable emotions, and make you waste a lot of the time you have alive. They use misunderstanding to shatter your good fortune and happiness, and even make you descend into empty illusory pain and suffering, so you feel that you have no strength to go on living. Only when you recognize the true mind, and abide in peace in the true mind, will you be able to get free of the deceptions and control of the false mind, and see through all false appearances, and directly reach the most plain and simple true characteristic.

To see the true mind, to recognize the true mind, to focus on the true mind, to preserve awareness of the true mind—this is what in Buddhism we call "becoming enlightened." After you become enlightened, the false mind still exists. It is like when a wave appears in the ocean, and the surface of the water is no longer flat as a mirror. The oceanic "true mind" is as even as the surface of a mirror, but when external objects are reflected in it, it is like the wind blowing and waves arising on the great ocean, and then false mind appears. When we use the power of wisdom or discipline to fend off the enticements of the external world and keep them outside the mind, the ocean of the mind slowly quiets down again. That state without waves or ripples is the true mind. When waves move in the mind, the false thoughts are born. When false thoughts stop, the true mind is revealed. For example, between this thought and the next thought, there is a state without thoughts. When you use your inherent nature or your mind of lucid awareness to observe it, it is very easy for you to merge with true mind.

After you are clear about the mind, all you have to do is preserve this true mind—that is the best cultivation. At this time, you must stay far away from the discriminating mind, and not let those concepts throw your mind into confusion. Cultivating practice in Buddhism implies cultivating the "true mind" — letting your inherent spark of wisdom that can ignite a prairie fire become the flame of wisdom, and burn away all your greed, anger, ignorance, arrogance, and doubt, until in the end all that is left is a single expanse of clear light. At this point you can finally be reckoned as having reached the ultimate achievement. What is the ultimate achievement? It is that nothing in this world can shake your tranquility and joy, and nothing can make you its slave. In other words, when you reach the ultimate achievement, you will have absolute freedom and happiness.

So then, how will you be able to see the true mind? The classic schools of Buddhism left us many expedient methods. For example, chanting the sutras and beating time on a wooden fish are to stabilize the mind, using cadence and rhythm to dissolve away false thoughts. When false thoughts dissolve, and you reach a kind of ultimate tranquility, you will see the true mind. The eighty-four thousand teaching methods in Buddhism are all for the purpose of enabling people to find this true mind. To choose which method to use, you must see which method is the most appropriate for you.

How Many People Can Make a Lucid Choice?

In human life, we should have a noble mind and spirit and attitude. We must be this way toward power, toward money, toward rank. While everyone in the world is scrambling after them, you must give them a slight smile. This is because what is called "independence" is not being trapped by thoughts and apparent forms, and you must not deliberately tie up and constrain your own mind.

One day I was talking with a young friend about the revelation of death. I told him that my younger brother had died when he was twenty-seven, and his death brought me a great shock and feeling of enlightenment. Even now, in the house in Wuwei (in Liangzhou) I still keep a headrest which is a dead man's skull, and this always reminds me that death can arrive at any time. After hearing this, my friend talked about how he was thinking three years earlier: he said that at the time his physical health was not good, and he realized that when he was healthy, he certainly would live the way he wanted to live. I asked him, "What kind of life do you want to lead?" He said, "Just like now, driving along the roads, often going on trips for several days." He also said that in fact he was already comparatively content with his present life, but he could never avoid feeling pain, and sometimes he would also feel some nameless dread for the future, and he would feel anger and sadness when other people misunderstood him and hurt him. I told him that what he needed was freedom, but not the kind of freedom he had now. Now he had only reached a kind of physical freedom, and although this kind of freedom is not bad, it is still something passive, because it requires material protection. If someday an economic crisis affected his company, his freedom would immediately be greatly reduced. What's more, since he often felt fear, anger, and sadness, this showed that having a certain material foundation had not brought him freedom of the mind and spirit.

In real life, many friends want to earn a lot of money, because they feel that this way they can achieve freedom and independence in life, but in fact it is often not like this. This is because the more they have, the more they see, and the more they do not want to lose it. The more they have and the more they long for, the more energy they must expend to maintain it and seek it. In this state of mind, it is very hard for them to realize freedom of the mind and spirit, and sometimes they have no way of preserving even the freedom of the body.

My students have had many experiences of this kind. For example, one student told me that in order to build a better living environment for her family, she was constantly making great efforts, and spent a great deal of her time working and socializing, and never listened patiently to her child, and never prepared a meal for her family. From an early age, her child lacked motherly love and attention, and became hypersensitive and suffered from an inferiority complex, and could not interact comfortably with other people. After the child grew up, she developed defects in her personality that were hard to repair. In contemporary society there are many such stories. Many children, from the time they are very small, are kept busy going to supplementary classes, and have no time to play, and no time to commune with nature. Little as they are, they are all carrying heavy book bags, wandering the streets alone. Every time I see this situation, I feel very saddened. I don't know whether or not one day all parents will be able to understand that what children need the most is not increasingly better material conditions, but rather love, attention, and correct guidance. But the many desires of the parents, along with the society's ever-changing values and views of life, are always polluting the children's minds and spirits, and pitilessly smashing their dreams and yearnings. They too will be like their parents, living harried lives under society's pressures, impossible to taste true happiness and freedom.

In reality, freedom is not as complicated as many people imagine. It is very plain and simple, and very pure. Moreover, it is not absolutely linked to material things. My son Chen Yixin's mother made an excellent statement: "Picking through the trash you can still manage to eat." She meant that a person must keep on living and it is not difficult. As long as a person can keep on living, he has the power to decide and choose his own manner of living. So what takes away your freedom is often not fate, but your mind filled with desire. Let's take an example. If you feel that in order to say you are living well, you must have a car and an apartment, and you must take an annual vacation abroad, then you have shackled yourself with invisible chains, because, to get these materials things you must give up a great deal, including the precious time you are alive, and sometimes what you give up will also include your standards for morality and virtue. What's more, your life is created by your mind, and if you do not have a mind and spirit that is free, then how can you live a free life?

I live very freely and happily, because I have given up many things. Many years ago, before I had become successful, I opened a bookstore, and that bookstore could earn a lot of money for me, but it was wasting a lot of my time, so without the least bit of hesitation, I closed it down. Many people who were in the book business with me have now become rich, but they all envy me, because I have produced many books, and more importantly, because I have left behind things that time cannot destroy. If I had wanted to eat well, dress well, live well, drive a car, then I would have only been able to do meaningless things. That's why I often say, in human life, we must always have a noble mind and spirit and attitude. We must be this way toward power, toward money, toward rank. While everyone in the world is scrambling after them, you must give them a slight smile. If you have this mind and spirit that is not bound by desires, then you will naturally be able to live freely and independently. This is because what is called "independence" is not being trapped by thoughts and apparent forms, and you must not deliberately tie up and constrain your own mind.

The liberation that Buddhists seek is a kind of absolute freedom — we also call it independence. It is not like the "freedom" that many people understand in theory. People usually think that the external world constrains their own words and actions, so they feel they are not free. But Buddhists recognize that freedom must be complete freedom, a realm of "total achievement in all directions." What's more, the freedom which Buddhists advocate is a freedom of the mind and spirit, a pure lucidity that is not deluded or confused by empty illusory apparent forms. It is the courage to make choices independently and firmly. It is not blind obstinate clinging, and not irresponsible indulgence. Nevertheless, there is an area where the "freedom" in people's mind and the "freedom" Buddhists speak of correspond. Both emphasize that we must "get free from bondage." But because there is a big difference between the Buddhist understanding of "bondage" and the common understanding of this term in society, this creates many divergences between how the two understand "freedom."

People all think that bondage is something the external world forces on them, and so they are accustomed to looking for the external world to change. But Buddhists think that bondage is the many clingings and attachments that arise from recognizing the false as true, and is something that people impose upon themselves. This is why what genuine Buddhist practitioners yearn for and seek is always a transformation of their own minds, and not a change in the external world. In their eyes, to genuinely "get free from bondage," they must leave behind all clingings and attachments.

Different points of view engender different choices, and different choices give rise to different results. I often say, the sun has the sun's trajectory, and a planet has a planet's trajectory. It is precisely all the differences that make up the abundance of the world. However, in this world, how many people can ultimately make lucid choices, and how many people are willing to accept all the results their choices bring?

True Freedom Is the Wakefulness of Wisdom

Freedom is not escape, it is not escaping from everything in the world that can create disturbances for the mind and spirit. Rather, it is letting a kind of wisdom that is inherent in life wake up, letting the light of this wisdom shine on your mind and spirit, and illuminate your life. Observing this inherent wisdom, you will spontaneously cut all the ties that bind your mind and spirit, and conquer all kinds of habit energies and false thoughts that block your mind and spirit, and see through to the real characteristic of the causes of suffering.

Worldly affairs are like fireworks. Every time fireworks are shot up into the sky, there are always people who give a loud shout. This is a false realm. When a false realm appears, we do not have to start using the mind that judges in terms of good and evil. If you are happy or sad when something happens, this is starting up with the mind of good and evil. This happens because you are unable to abide in peace in the empty inherent nature, and you are unable to abide in peace in the true mind. When you do not abide in peace in the true mind, minor things can make your mind and feelings change a lot. For example, you were just very happy, but suddenly someone rebukes you, and at this your mind immediately fills with anger. You do not understand that when someone else rebukes you, this is a temporary emotion, and your being rebuked is just a memory. If you abide in peace in the true mind, and you are not concerned with anything, then nobody can rebuke you, and nobody can take away your happiness and tranquility.

I often send friends a short note I have written myself: Always be clearly aware in the here and now; whatever you encounter, go along with circumstances; be happy and free from sorrow. Doing things is like painting space with colors: while you are painting, focus your attention, and after you have painted, let it go. In the mind and in emptiness, there are no cares or worries. This is the classic letting things take their course, and being relaxed and calm. Letting things take their course is going along with nature, being free and independent. Being relaxed and calm means that the mind is totally calm, without any anxieties, and without any vexations. If a person can thoroughly carry out the point I express in this short note, the person will achieve true freedom.

This kind of freedom is easier said than done. Why ? Because people who grow up in an ignorant social environment are like children who have grown up in a pack of wolves — they cannot change the wolf cub energy they have had their whole lives. Through longtime conditioning, mistaken viewpoints have become maggots on meat. They have merged into our lives, transformed our sense of values, our views on human life and the world, even our moral standards. Therefore, even if we understand some theoretical truth, we will always see everything in the world as very real. We especially see our bodies as things that really exist. What the eyes see, what the ears hear, what the nose smells, what the tongue tastes, what the body touches, what the brain thinks of—all of these things are deceiving us, and we are afflicted by all kinds of clinging and attachment, and we get farther and farther away from peaceful tranquility and clear illumination. This is why Laozi said in the *Dao De Jing, The Book of the Path and Its Power*: "For the sake of the Path, reduce this, and keep on reducing it and reducing it, in order to get to the point that there is no contrived action, and with no contrived action, nothing is left undone." The meaning of this saying is that we must energetically clear away the filth from our minds and spirits, until we have removed all our ideas of material gain, and dissolved away all desires, and reached a state where there is no seeking: only then will our true mind send forth its crystalline pure clear light. When we abide in peace in the true mind, whatever we do, whatever we think, it is all the wondrous functioning of the true mind. Only then can we do things without clinging and being attached to them, only then can we taste without greedy longing. No matter what we do, it will always be without calculating the results, and no more will it produce afflictions.

Unfortunately, many people do not understand this point. They accept the false as true, and cannot see through to the true characteristic of affliction, and they are greedy for the various pleasures of the world. They are unwilling to be like the people who cultivate practice, to lead a regulated and pure life: they feel that such a life would inevitably be boring and insipid. But they do not know that this kind of life holds within it the bliss of a plain and simple tranquility. The bliss of this tranquility is also a poetic feeling, a kind of ecstasy that goes beyond material gain. The happiness of this cannot be compared with ordinary happiness, and it is something that nothing in the world can shake. Thus we say, although there are many kinds of affliction, when we get to the bottom of it all, there is just one basic cause that produces affliction: that is "not clearly understanding."

Once people do not clearly understand, they will make mistakes by going against the correct principles, and invert the root and the branch. It was because of this that the *Heart Sutra* says: "Far removed from inverted dreamlike thinking is ultimate nirvana." What does it mean by inverted dreamlike thinking? First, not to understand the true principle of impermanence, and to accept the false as the true. Second, to be greedy for worldly pleasure, and not understand that desire is the source of suffering. Third, not to understand that everything in the world is empty, illusory, and impermanent, and that there are no differences in basic substance, and because of this, to give rise to many dualistic false thoughts. Fourth, not to understand that the "self" is also something created by the coming together of causal conditions, and has no intrinsic nature, and will not last forever. In other words, what the sutra calls "inverted dreamlike thinking" is accepting the false as the true, and clinging to illusion as reality.

I often say to students: "If you do not have the great death, then you will not have the great birth. If you do not have great pain, then you will not have great peace." This is just because a person's life is filled with various kinds of inverted confused views and interpretations. Among these, most to be feared is conventional happiness, whose basic substance is suffering, and to accept it as genuine happiness. This is because when a person feels happiness, the person will not want to change anything. Conversely, when a person encounters suffering and difficulty, and experiences setbacks that the person is unwilling to accept, the person seeks to make changes, and begins to think and reflect: only then will there be different degrees of growth. When devastation attacks, this is what I call "the great death," and it will allow people to completely let go of all their clingings and attachments to everything in the world. It will let them recognize the true mind, and see empty inherent nature, and gain genuine freedom and liberation. From this point they will live happily and without worries, and so, contrary to how it might seem, this is a "great birth."

Sadly, for some people, even when they meet with devastating blows, like the loss of their spouses, or a terminal illness, they still cannot completely awaken, and instead choose to live for the moment, and indulge their desires even more than they did before. Without a doubt they are totally wasting their chance for liberation.

The true enemy of tranquility, of joy, of independence is desire; it is not the external world. If you cannot give up the various greedy cravings in your mind, even if you escape far into the mountain forests and cultivate practice in seclusion, you still will not be able to avoid calculating and scheming. This is why there can be so many monks who, despite wearing monastic robes, still have minds that are full of greedy desires, clingings, and attachments. Moreover, to want to escape from everything in the mundane world and rely on the purity of the wilderness to recover your tranquility is a kind of passivity and selfishness. Lama Thangtong Gyalpo (a Shangpa Kagyu master teacher, 1361–1485) criticized the many practitioners who escaped to the mountain valleys to cultivate practice and did not care about the hardships suffered by the common folk.

Thus we say that freedom is not escape. It is not escaping from everything in the world that can create disturbances for the mind and spirit. Rather, it is letting this wisdom that is inherent in life wake up—it is letting the light of this wisdom shine on your mind and spirit, and illuminate your life. Observing this inherent wisdom, you will spontaneously cut all the ties that bind your mind and spirit, and conquer all kinds of habit energies and false thoughts that block your mind and spirit, and see through to the real characteristic of the causes of suffering. Then, even if you taste the fruit of suffering, in your mind there will no longer be any distinction between suffering and happiness. If you are this way, then there is no way for affliction to be produced.

When you train your mind and spirit according to the Dharma day after day, and you enter into a state of tranquility, and you are constantly observing all the changes in your inner mind, you will gradually discover that true happiness and independence really do not require any external conditions, they are just a state of the mind and spirit. When you constantly preserve this state of tranquility, happiness, and lucidity, you will discover that everything in the world is flowing by like a burbling stream of water, because what comes together also scatters again, and what scatters also comes together again. This includes your false thoughts and emotions, which become fewer and fewer — they are also empty, illusory, and impermanent.

Oftentimes, in the instant that you concentrate, your calculations and the thoughts you care about spontaneously dissolve away, so you do not feel like going on calculating anything, caring about anything, seeking anything that is already changing, or expecting anything that has not happened yet. You would rather value something while you have it, and give it a reason to last longer, and when you cannot get it or you lose it, you let it go. You are not reluctant to part with things, and you do not expectantly await things. You just concentrate on the present moment, and savor it. One day you will discover that even liberation and reaching the other shore are no longer on your mind, and there is nothing in this world that can change your mind. At this time you finally experience thorough enlightenment. Thorough enlightenment is true freedom.

Freedom Is a Matter of Mind in Accord with Mind

If you reach accord with a certain mystic power of the universe, you can enter into a whole new state of living, a state of independence of body and mind, without any concerns. So then, what is this certain mystic power of the universe? Is it the spirit of great good and great beauty? Is it great love? It is, but it is not only this.

How can we who yearn for freedom experience the awakening of wisdom? This requires that we "reach accord" with a certain great spirit of the universe. What does it mean, to "reach accord?" Reaching accord is "mind in accord with mind." The untitled verse by the Tang dynasty poet Li Shangyin gives the most spiritually alive footnote to the phrase "mind in accord with mind."

Having no wings, I Cant't fly to you as I please;
Our hearts at one, your ears can heard my inner call.

What a beautiful poem. It expresses what, in love, is hardest to describe in words, and is also something beautiful and wondrous. It is a kind of spiritual mystery, and it is also a kind of indescribable, unexplainable resonance that comes from the depths of the soul.

When two souls that love each other reach resonance, one moment of eye contact can connect the two of them, and then all is quiet, and the whole world becomes something empty that exists in name only, and all that is left in the boundless universe are the two joined minds. It is as if you can hear your partner's breathing, her heartbeat, and every subtle thought. The sound of her inner mind resonates in your inner mind, and because of the merging of spirits, you feel relaxed and in harmony, and filled with an indescribable joy. At the same time, in your eyes, this world that has been like a stage set is no longer something lifeless. It has a pulse, and its body is growing — the earth, the plants, the mountains, the lakes, everything has all become alive. You can hear the quiet voices and laughter of all things, you can see their joy and their silence, you can feel their grief and their losses. You will no longer feel empty and bored, because you and your love have completely merged in a place deep within your inner minds. She is there in you, and you are there in her. You are her, and she is you. Time and space are no longer a problem, and the electric current of the soul lets the two of you penetrate through time and space, and feel each other. This complete harmony of souls, like mixing water and milk, sends people into rapture even more than physical contact. You will feel that your lover is the key that links you to the mind of the universe. Through your spiritual resonance with her, you experience the most beautiful part of love, and you will feel that you are willing to give everything, including your life, to let her experience good fortune and happiness. You will feel that the grandeur of this love will even let you love the whole world, and you will feel a "perfect fusion" as you have never had before. This is arriving at the love of "reaching accord."

This kind of love will realize the highest aspirations of the human race for true love. It can make people feel happiness even more than the satisfactions of physical desire, like the desire to possess, to control, and so on. Because desire is endless, seeking what you desire and not getting it brings a pain that bores into the mind, and when you have what you desire, you will be afraid of losing it. Worldly love unavoidably brings people suffering. When you mistakenly think that satisfying desires is more important than spiritual accord, it will be impossible to achieve stability, and reach the "accord" of love. You will inevitably be afflicted by being lovesick, and to make this kind of "love" last forever, you will stop at nothing. Don't you know that the physical body ultimately decays, so how can anything based on the physical body last forever? You will feel hopeless because of the gap between expectations and reality. Satisfying desires will bring you empty glory, like dewdrops on the leaves, which will evaporate totally in an instant. Sometimes all that is left in your mind is a sense of loss and emptiness, and you feel very lonely. You ask the world that how can love bring such sweetness, and also bring such suffering? Can this be the truth of love? In reality, you should not ask the world about this — what you should ask about it is your own mind and spirit. Can it be that the heavenly feelings you experienced did not come from a complete merging? This kind of merging enables you to feel that she is the person you have been looking for your whole life, that she is the one who knows you, that she is your soulmate. She brought to life your courage, your resolve, all your positive feelings toward life. You may even feel that it was only because of her that you became a complete person, and not just an empty body, an animal that only knows how to find food and seek pleasure. She enabled you to have higher yearnings, and made you understand the truth of life.

If you have clearly understood all the metaphors above, then you have clearly understood the beauty and wonder of souls merging, and you may yearn for this kind of endless, infinite poetic feeling. It is an enchanting feeling that comes after you have forgotten about mundane practical concerns. It is very similar to genuine faith. Within this poetic feeling, there is no petty self, and no individual gain and loss, and no more dualism and discriminating thought. When you love not just one woman, but the whole human race, all living spirits, and even the whole cosmos, your love ascends from the level of conventional worldly love and becomes a kind of faith, a great love. Why do we call it great love? Great love is an attitude of selfless service. Its difference from petty love lies in the fact that the object of great love is the whole universe, all living beings, and not only one particular woman or man, or kinfolk related to you by blood. All faiths have something like great love, though everyone has a different name for it. For example, in Buddhism they call great love "unconditional great compassion that shares the same essence with all beings." In the West they prefer to call it "universal love."

A girl once wrote a little poem that won universal praise. It went like this:

Whether you see me or not
I am there
Not sad, not happy
Whether you think of me or not
The feeling is there
It doesn't come and it doesn't go
Whether you love me or not
Love is there
It doesn't increase and it doesn't decrease
Whether you are with me or not
My hand is in your hand
Not letting go

Many people think this is a sentimental poem, but in fact, what it speaks of is the true mind that accompanies us from lifetime to lifetime, the light of inherent wisdom in sentient beings. One of my students had a very good description of it. He said what this poem conveys is the feeling of a kind of Buddhist romanticism. It truly is that way. Buddhism is not like so many people think it is, cold and lifeless. The true mind we speak of, the inherent original mind, is not something heartless. Although Buddhism recognizes that everything is empty illusion, and not worth caring about, nevertheless Buddha was concerned for all living beings. This is something on a grander scale than the concerns men and women have for each other; it is the very great spirit of Buddhism, the spirit of compassion that benefits living beings. When a man loves a woman deeply, he can sacrifice his life for her. But when it comes to the buddhas and bodhisattvas, they care more about the suffering of any living being than their own lives. This is why there are stories of the Buddha "cutting off pieces of his own flesh to feed the eagles, and sacrificing his body to feed the tigers." We cannot deny that this is a more beautiful vista than some petty love.

Buddhist wisdom recognizes that if you are in accord with a certain mystic power of the universe, you will be able to enter into a whole new state of living, a state where body and mind are independent, and there you have absolutely no worries. So then, what is that certain mystic power of the universe? Is it the spirit of great good and great beauty? Is it great love? It is, but it is not only this. Besides great love, this spiritual power also contains an ultimate wisdom. And when great love merges with this ultimate wisdom, it forms "the Path." The eighty-four thousand teaching methods of Buddhism are all to let you reach accord with "the Path." Only when you reach accord with the Path will you be able to manage your own mind, and enable it to reach the place it must reach. This is also the fundamental meaning of meditation.

The Bright True Mind Is Always with You

*The only thing that does not change is your true mind.
It is the "observer" in the world of your inner mind that
knows when you are cold, when you are getting old, and
when afflictions arise. It is something that exists that is
pure and lucid like a bright mirror, and unshakeable as a
diamond. It will not change, nor will it be damaged. It is
like a clear bright sky and a still quiet ocean. It alone can
really be there with you always.*

We know that change is the true characteristic of this world.
Everything in this world is constantly changing, including the
seemingly eternal sun, moon, and stars. Some people are aware of
this, and feel that when humans are alive they endure suffering,
because nothing they have can last forever: their feelings of love,
everything they have worked at so hard, their reputations, their
cars, their apartments, their parents and spouses and children,
even their own lives. They very much want to know whether or
not there is anything that will not change.

There is, but there also is not. We say there is, because

Buddhism recognizes that there is one state that is eternal — this state is called "the diamond mind." We say there is not, because the diamond mind is not a concrete material object, and even if you look in every corner of the whole world, you will not find a thing called "the diamond mind." The diamond mind is the indestructible true mind; it has no beginning and no end, and is neither born nor extinguished.

Buddhist wisdom recognizes that although everything in this world is illusory transformation and unreal and impermanent, nevertheless, the wisdom that can perceive the law of impermanence is not "inert emptiness" — it is the inherent true mind of living beings, the fundamental original mind. Change is the immutable truth. Everything in the world is undergoing changes, and is all changing every moment — but this truth of "change" does not change, and the awareness that lets you experience this truth does not change either. What is this awareness? It is our recognition of the truth. This truth itself is a kind of law inherent in nature — it is impermanence.

The true mind that can recognize the truth of impermanence always accompanies all living spirits. No matter how many times our living bodies experience the cycle of birth and death, and how many times we go through the process from being born to being destroyed, or how we are transformed from this embodiment into another embodiment, this true mind never leaves us. Even if we do not understand it clearly, it is always there. You cannot see it, but it really exists. It has no beginning, and it has no so-called end. It cannot be defiled by the ashes and dust of false thoughts, and it cannot be called "clean or unclean." It cannot be increased, and it cannot be reduced. It is the spiritual nature hidden in the depths of your inner mind. It is the basis for you to transcend life, and even transcend birth and death, and realize liberation. When you have recognized it, you spontaneously accept the impermanence of the world. You discover that although change is painful, it is also the causal basis for you to be able to live independently. This is because everything that seems real, including what your eyes see, what your ears hear, what your nose smells, what your body touches, and all the thoughts in your brain—all of these things are the many apparent forms that appear after the myriad material causes and conditions come together. We cannot say that they never existed, but they return to empty inherent nature, empty and illusory and impermanent. When the previous causal conditions disperse, they immediately change.

Let's take a simple example. Did the wild animal you saw in a dream exist? In actual fact, it does not exist, but in the dream, it did really exist, and you were mangled and mauled by it, and could not get away. In your memory, it also really existed, and after you woke up, you still knew that you had dreamed of something frightening. But when the dreams and the memories dissolve away, it too dissolves away.

In fact, the so-called real world is also this way. It is not substantially different from a dream. These are all things formed by the coming together of causal conditions, and when the causal conditions disperse, they dissolve away, and when new causal conditions come together, they are transformed into another shape. For example, when you turn left at a crossroads, you see a female student carrying a book bag on her back. You brush by her, and then she exists in your world. But she immediately becomes a memory, and you may soon forget her. Once you have forgotten her, in your world she has disappeared forever. If you understand its real substance, her existence was only something like a dream or illusion. Take another example. You speak of a deep love that you will remember all your life, but one day your partner no longer loves you, and after a few years you end up not caring anymore, and then you discover that that past sweet tenderness was like a dream. Even the girl you loved seems like someone in a dream. The way she thinks has changed, and her attitude toward you has changed, and she is no longer that girl you loved, and of course, you yourself have changed. Another example. You see a very pretty girl and you have a good feeling toward her, and so you focus your attention on her. You wait for an opportunity to get to know her, and you even fantasize about many beautiful things that will take place between you two. As Tolstoy said in *Anna Karenina*, "The whole universe is waiting for the signal to be sent." But she suddenly spits out a mouthful of phlegm on the ground. You are abruptly turned off, and all your fantasies are destroyed, and the good feeling you had for her immediately evaporate like dewdrops in the hot sun, and nothing remains.

Obviously, everything in the world is constantly changing, so it's like one dream after another, like a stream of water whooshing by. It goes on changing, and has never stopped.

The only thing that does not change is your true mind. It is the "observer" in the world of your inner mind that knows when you are cold, when you are getting old, and when afflictions arise. It is something that exists that is pure and lucid like a bright mirror, and unshakeable as a diamond. It will not change, nor will it be damaged. It is like a clear bright sky and a still quiet ocean. It alone can really be there with you always.

Nevertheless, it is not that everyone can discover its existence. It is like us being unable to see a white hair appearing on the top of our heads. If at this time someone tells you, "You have a white hair on the top of your head," you will lower your head and look in the mirror, and try to find it, and only then might you be able to see it. The person who told you that you have grown a white hair (the teacher), the mirror (the teaching), and the appropriate physical position (real practice) — these are the causal conditions that allow you to recognize true mind. When all the causal conditions come together and start to function together, you will open to enlightenment, and discover your own inherent true mind. Thus it is said that recognizing true mind is also a phenomenon brought about by the coming together of causal conditions. People who do not clearly understand the true mind can only go through the teachings, and do all they can to build up favorable conditions for illuminating mind and seeing its true nature. But if opportune conditions do not come, trying to force it only adds to a person's afflictions.

For example, before you read this book or knew me, maybe you did not understand Buddhist wisdom, and you did not recognize the possibility that you would have ultimate liberation. But one day, your friend recommended that you read this book. In this book I have described a kind of absolute freedom and happiness, and you believe me, and a great yearning arises in your mind. In this state of great yearning, you faithfully put into practice what I am explaining here, and then maybe one day you will personally experience the kind of feeling I am talking about.

Thus we say, although the true mind is neither born nor destroyed, and is with us lifetime after lifetime; still, whether or not we can discover it, when we discover it, and how we discover it, must depend on causal conditions. "Practicing according to causal conditions" is one of the Buddhist methods of cultivating practice. What it emphasizes is not forcibly seeking, but rather spontaneously adapting, going along with causal conditions, not giving rise to arbitrary notions of good and evil, not altering your mental state following the birth and demise of apparent phenomena. It is a wondrous teaching of using things and events to cultivate and refine the mind and spirit, and it is also wisdom exercising its function in the midst of life.

Take Hold of the Opportunity, and Welcome the Awakening of the Spiritual Nature

Everything in the world is a part of emptiness. It is born in emptiness, and is extinguished in emptiness. Everything in the world, including ourselves, is to the emptiness just as the ocean spray is to the ocean.

All that you constantly perceive — is your body perceiving this, or is your mind and spirit perceiving this? If it is your body perceiving, why is it that in dreams you still have very realistic sensations of touch, of smell, of vision, of acting and speaking? Why do you still have joy and fear and sorrow, a sense of good fortune and a sense of loss? Why is it that you almost cannot distinguish the boundary between dreams and real life? Obviously, a person's life is not just a life of bodily perceptions, it is also a life of your mind and spirit perceiving. As long as the six sense faculties (eyes, ears, nose, tongue, body, conceptual mind) can function, you will be able to hear many sounds, and when your fingers hit the keyboard, you will have the corresponding sense of touch, and when you open your eyes you will be able to see everything around you, and you will be able to smell the scent of flowers and the earthy odors wafting in from afar. But all these are illusory transformations without inherent nature: they cannot go forever without changing, and they are undergoing transformations every minute. Thus, there is no distinction in substance between this and that, no distinction in time, no distinction between good and bad, no distinction between beautiful and ugly, no distinction between good to hear and not good to hear, no distinction between far and near, no distinction between large and small... When you clearly understand this point, you will discover that your own mind is the same as the external world — it is all illusory transformation, and both return to the empty inherent nature. At this point you will spontaneously eliminate the dualistic opposition between the "self" and the external world, and reach what Buddhism calls the state of "one flavor." This is a state where everything is truly equal. Then all the appearances in the world are fused into your light of wisdom.

Let's consider an example. Ocean spray is an apparent form that happens by chance, and it cannot represent the whole of the ocean. But there is no difference in substance between the spray and the ocean: the spray is part of the ocean, and it can merge into one body with the ocean. Therefore, you cannot take the ocean and the spray and see them as two opposed things. When you understand this point, you will discover that everything in the world is part of emptiness. It is born in emptiness, and is extinguished in emptiness. Everything in the world, including ourselves, is to the emptiness just as the ocean spray is to the ocean.

You may still not understand this explanation, because you might feel that humans and ocean sprays cannot be the same thing, that ocean sprays disappear very quickly, while human life lasts a lot longer. In fact, time and the myriad things and events are the same — they are all empty and illusory and impermanent. Let's take a simple example. When you are with a person you love, you always feel that time passes quickly, but when you are with someone you are sick and tired of, you always feel that time goes by extremely slowly. By the same reasoning, a human lifetime to us is not a few decades, but only a few unforgettable moments. When we are facing death, we always feel that we only lived those few moments. No matter when we come to the end of our lives, we always feel that we still have not yet lived enough, and there are still so many things we want to do, and so many things we cannot give up. This is why we say that time too is an illusory perception.

When you discover that you are like a wave in the ocean, and both are illusory perceptions, you will understand what a preposterous idea it is to want to hold onto something forever, and especially to seek something insistently, regardless of the methods and the costs. This is because, if even "I" am an illusion, is there anything that will be "mine" forever?

If you genuinely understand this truth, then you will not insistently seek so many things, and you will look upon everything neutrally. You will no longer care how other people judge you, and you will no longer care whether or not you possess anything. You will only focus on the direction you sincerely believe in, and you will make this neutrality and this steadfastness your means for living life and dealing with the world. At this point, you will naturally become the master of your own mind and spirit.

Preserving this clear lucid awareness, and staying detached like an onlooker, will enable your mind to increase in scope day by day, and no longer discriminate among the many things you experience in terms of gain and loss and pain and pleasure, and instead only use the various kinds of life experience to complete your own knowledge of the world. Then day by day you will be more able to understand the various kinds of people and events, and day by day you will get closer to the truth of life. Bit by bit you will dissolve away that self constructed of illusory forms, and what is derived from this self: greed, anger, ignorance, arrogance, and doubt. One day you will discover that, in reality, no separation exists between that clear lucid awareness and that onlooker, and that there no longer exists anything that must be dismissed from your mind, or any questions that must be clarified. You will discover that although the texture of the world is intricate and complex, it is as clear as the lines in the palm of your hand.

At this point, even if your body stays in somewhere noisy and chaotic, or in someplace very dangerous, you will still be tranquil, happy, and focused, and your mind and spirit will abide in peace at every moment in a state that is relaxed but clearly awake. You will understand that nothing that happens in the external world can throw your mind into confusion. This empty quiet clear bright mind is what we call the true mind.

If you believe in its plainness and simplicity, if you believe that both ordinary people and sages possess it, if you wipe away all arrogance and doubt, and you use your mind and spirit to contact the truth, then gradually you will be able to personally taste its flavor, and at this time, you too will wake up.

When you really wake up, you see clearly the interconnections between life and the world. You will have no doubts about anything, and you will arrive at a true state of "no confusion." Because of this, you will not only be able to deal appropriately with everything in life, but also be filled with compassion and selfless love toward the whole world. This is because you know that the tragedies brought about by ignorance are being played out every minute on the stage of the world, but the great majority of the players have no way of drawing nutrition from these tragedies. They make the same mistakes over and over again, and get tangled up in the webs they weave. For example, the continuous rise in the material level of life requires more and more energy sources to support it, and to obtain more and more energy sources, conflicts break out among the human race under all sorts of pretexts. Even more frightening, in order to seek immediate profits, and a level of consumption that is a bit better than the present one, we do not hesitate to gamble with the future of humanity. We develop the power that can destroy everything, like nuclear power. After you wake up, you will clearly understand all this, but you will also know at a deep level that only if people are willing to face their own minds directly, make contact with the truth, and go on to change their minds and spirits, will there be the possibility of changing their lives and fates. All the powers that come from outside are just the "cooperative conditions." To cure the sickness, people must believe and be willing to swallow the bitter medicine.

When you have understood this, you will understand why in my novel *The Spells of Xixia*, when Grandfather Jiu, the man of great achievement (the man who transcends ordinary life and enters sagehood), confronts the plague that is spreading through the villages, just sings and dances together with five girls who are the transformed bodies of dakinis (beings who are like goddesses). They continuously sing of the truth of impermanence:

Mountains and rivers and the great earth
Are fundamentally the coming together of causal conditions.
Though they appear in all sorts of shapes and colors,
If we look for their inherent nature, they have none.
We offer this advice to the people of the world:
See through to the true face.

Don't be bound by clinging and possessions,
Give up anger and wrath,
Alas, how sad!
We'd better make an effort.
We offer this advice to the people of the world:
Why must you be so ignorant and deluded?
The myriad objects are empty in an instant,
The myriad objects cannot be taken away.
Why don't you come along with us,
Laughing and happy?

It's Not That You Resolve a Question, It's That There Is No Question

Why would you rather rely on alcohol or cigarettes or marijuana or even heroin, and be unwilling to go forward and welcome the awakening of wisdom? Wisdom when awakened is like the fundamental spiritual light inherent in your life, and it will influence your life without you being aware of it.

Truth has many names in Buddhism. Sometimes it is called "the good," sometimes it is called "the beautiful," sometimes it is called "love." But this is not necessarily goodness, beauty, and love in the ordinary sense, and so these terms are often accompanied by the word "great"—as in great good, great beauty, great love. Strictly speaking, this word "great" is not a relative dualistic concept, but rather a description of a certain realm of experience. It is similar to terms in the *Dao De Jing*: "great form without form," "great sound without sound," and so on. It signifies that after the greatness of the myriad things reaches a certain degree, there are no limits or external forms. This kind of greatness is like the boundlessness of the universe.

In some linguistic systems, they give the Buddhist idea of truth another name — the Tao, (which means "the Path" or "the Way.") But again, this is not the same as the usual path; rather, it is the ultimate Path, the light of inherent wisdom. This light is also called the true mind. The true mind is not the same as what we speak of in the Chinese phrase "true mind, genuine intent" (which means "genuinely and sincerely" or "with all my heart"). What is the distinction between the two? The former, "true mind" in the Buddhist sense, is a pure clear state far removed from all false thoughts. The latter, "true mind" in the everyday colloquial Chinese phrase, just means not being false with someone, not lying or cheating. Not being false in this sense means that in your mind there is still a dualism of true and false. But in the world of true mind, no dualism exists. Speaking from the true meaning, when the ordinary person says "true mind," it is only what is true at this moment, and what is true at this moment will quickly change into a moment of falsity, because the myriad things are constantly changing.

Let me give an example. At this moment you feel you are very much alone, and you do not love anyone, and you are not loved by anyone. But the next moment, suddenly someone calls you on the phone, and asks how you have been lately, and talks a lot about what is on his mind. At this moment, you may totally forget about the negative emotion you were feeling just a moment ago, and feel that you love someone and that you are loved. This is why we say that be it words or feelings, it is all impermanent. In this world nothing can last forever, and so there cannot exist anything that is the ultimate truth, and there cannot be anything that is ultimately false. In other words, the ultimate truth is that there is only "change," and correspondingly, the ultimate falsehood is that something is "permanent."

Not acting falsely cannot enable you to find the true mind, because your clinging to notions of true and false will keep you far away from the true mind. The true mind is far removed from all concepts and logic, and far removed from all dualistic oppositions. If you cling to any concepts or logic — including what I am expressing about the true mind — it will always take you far away from the genuine true mind, which is also the "empty inherent nature" that Buddhism is always talking about. You must certainly understand that it is not something you invent, but rather something you discover. Thus, there is no way for you to make it up: all you can do is see it.

When you manage to see the empty inherent nature, this is "awakening to the Path," and it is also called "seeing the Path." What kind of process is this then? I'll give you an example. One day a friend gives you the key to his house. You find his house based on the address, open the door, and turn on the light switch at the door. The dark room immediately lights up, and at the same time, you clearly see the "true face" of his house. Previously many people had described it to you from many points of view, in many forms: that there were three chairs in the right corner, and the wall paper was pale yellow, and the curtains were country-style, and so on. But in your brain, it had never been possible to form a realistic, concrete image of the house. Thus, the instant you turn on the light, yon have a feeling of sudden awakening: "Ah, actually it is like this." It is also this way when you see empty inherent nature, when you see the original face of the world.

When you manage to see the original face of the world, you will understand the law by which the myriad things operate. When you take this moment of clear understanding and let it soak into the genes of your life, it will operate everywhere at all times, enabling you to spontaneously eliminate clingings and afflictions. I'll give you a simple example. If you have met Xuemo, you will not be fooled by an imposter who also has a big beard, and even if you do not use your reason to analyze it, you will surely be able to see through the lies in the mouth of the fake "Xuemo." By the same principle, once you have clearly understood that everything before your eyes is all made up of the coming together of causal conditions, that it is all changing, then you will not cling to any false form of permanence, or desperately seek something that cannot last forever and try to make it last forever. Naturally you will greatly reduce afflictions. But this kind of clear understanding is not "clear understanding" at the verbal level. Even if you understand what this sentence means, as soon as you encounter something, it is very possible that you will forget all the principles I have been explaining. Thus, intellectual knowledge does not equal wisdom, and it cannot affect your life. If you want to genuinely liberate your own life from pain and suffering, you must genuinely perceive this truth, and see this answer. You cannot rely on alcohol or cigarettes or television shows. Why? Because their effects cannot last forever, and it is very possible that they will damage your physical body. If you rely on such things to numb your afflictions, and release the pressures you feel, once they lose their effectiveness, the afflictions and pressures will return to your exhausted body and mind, and make you suffer endless pain. So why would you rather rely on alcohol or cigarettes or marijuana or even heroin, and be unwilling to go forward and welcome the enlightenment of wisdom?

Enlightened wisdom is like the inherent spiritual light in your life, and it will influence your life without you knowing it. You do not have to deliberately remind yourself, yet you will spontaneously discover that in the world, no questions have to be resolved, and no one is opposed to you, and everything is a stage prop for refining your mind and spirit. Everything you go through is enriching your life experience, making you more profound and happy. In your mind there will be no more unsatisfied desires and cravings, no more resentments, and you will spontaneously live independently and at ease. From this point on, every move you make will elucidate the truth of great good and great beauty, and everything you say and do will be a genuine manifestation of the Buddha Dharma. You will never again ask me, "What is great beauty? How beautiful is great beauty?" because your own mind will already be filled with great beauty. You will never again ask me, "How good is great good? Why is it distinguished from lesser good?" because your own mind will already be filled with great good. You will never again ask me, "What is great love? How much love is great love?" because your own mind will already be filled with great love. You will not have the least bit of doubt or confusion or hesitation or uncertainty about how to proceed, because you will spontaneously know how you should do things without thinking or guessing or calculating.

A student once asked me: "What is the wondrous observing wisdom (one of the four wisdoms of the enlightened ones)? I am always observing other people, and from this I analyze the psychological motives behind their actions and behavior. Is this the wondrous observing wisdom or not?" I told her that this is a kind of intelligence. Intelligent people understand analysis and judgment, but they cannot yet genuinely see through things. This is because genuine insight is not intelligence, but rather the wondrous functioning of wisdom. For example, when you are walking outside, when your body begins to get wet, you know that it could be about to rain, and you must open your umbrella—is there some thought process in this? There's not. This is more of a direct feeling.

Take another example: you love your mother from the bottom of your heart, and this love even goes beyond the love you feel for yourself. So do you still have to read a book like "How to Get Along With Your Mother" before you can guarantee you will not do anything to hurt your mother? No, you don't, because you hope she can have good fortune and happiness, and you cannot bear to let her worry or lose hope, so how could you do anything to hurt her? Thus we say that you must not take intelligence for wisdom, and you must not take cleverness for wisdom.

If you want to know the meaning of Buddhist terms like the *wondrous observing wisdom*, the *wisdom of the essential nature of the realm of reality*, the *great mirror wisdom,* the *wisdom to accomplish actions*, the *wisdom of inherent equality*, you must properly cultivate your own mind and spirit, and enable mind and spirit to slowly come to possess a certain focus, a certain tranquility, so that in the world where there are myriad changes every moment, you cultivate a realm that is without moving. Then, without having to think about it, you will know the three bodies and five wisdoms that Buddhism teaches about. The foregoing descriptions all are like the finger pointing at the moon: they are not the moon itself, and they are not wisdom itself.

Section Three:

Find Your True Enemy

We Have So Many Misunderstandings of the World and of Life

When you recognize the true mind, and you can preserve the true mind, and you reach the level where you do not waver, this is nirvana. When you do not clearly understand the true mind, and you are confused about the here and now, and confused about the external world, and always worried about external things, this is samsara.

What does it mean not to clearly understand? It means being unable to clearly see the true characteristic, to accept the false as true, to cling to the illusory as real, to be deluded and confused and led astray by apparent forms that suddenly appear and disappear—this is not clearly understanding. Because we do not clearly understand, we produce desires; because we have desires, we produce clingings and attachments; because we have clingings and attachments, we produce afflictions.

No matter what we do, no matter what manner of life we choose, it is all in order to attain happiness, peace, a sense of ease and independence, but these are all perceptions of the mind. Even if our apartments and cars and money and all the rest of it can let us live very comfortably, and enable us to attain the satisfactions of empty success, these things cannot enable us to attain lasting happiness. Why not? Because they themselves do not last forever. The satisfaction of empty glory is a feeling that very quickly dissolves away. Whether you live comfortably or not depends on what demands you have on life, and apartment buildings, cars, money and all such things are always changing. Apartment buildings can get old. They can be used for about seventy years, and we cannot say for sure when they will be demolished, not to mention wiped out by an earthquake or a flood. Cars have an even shorter lifespan. Though the lifetime of money is comparatively longer, everything you can buy with it has a limited lifespan, and the value of currency is constantly changing. That's why we say that material things are impermanent, and all kinds of happiness and comfort based on material conditions are impermanent. Despite this, we are not willing to seek unconditional happiness, independence, ease and peace. On the contrary, we take those empty, illusory, unreal things as the goal of human life, at the price of happiness and good health, and heedlessly pursue them. The contradiction in this clearly indicates that we will have to accept the sufferings and vexations that these mistaken choices bring us.

Why can't we be clear about what we need? Why do we keep mistaking the false for the true? It is because we have too many misunderstandings of life and the world. If you carefully observe every detail in life, you will discover that many contradictions are brought about by misunderstandings. Rifts produced by misunderstandings can come about even between the people we are closest to, including parents and companions, and may even get to the point where we have nothing more to do with them until they grow old and die. It is obvious that misunderstandings are very much to be feared.

What are misunderstandings? They are false thoughts. Where then does our false mind come from? False mind is formed by the coming together of the three causal conditions: sense faculties, sense objects, and consciousness. Our bodies have six sense faculties: (in Buddhist terms,) the eyes are the sense faculty of the eyes, the ears are the sense faculty of the ears, the nose is the sense faculty of the nose, the tongue is the sense faculty of the tongue, the body is the sense faculty of the body, the conceptual mind is the sense faculty of the conceptual mind. Given these six sense faculties, six kinds of consciousness are produced, and then this gives rise to the six sense objects: form, sound, scent, flavor, touch, conceptualized things. The false mind is produced by the coming together of the causal conditions of your six sense faculties and six sense consciousnesses with the external world. When your eyes see that a woman is beautiful, it gives rise to false mind, and you want to get to know her. This is the result of the functioning produced by the sense faculty of the eyes, and the visual consciousness, and the external environment.

The great majority among us have had no awakening yet, and have not recognized the true mind. Because of this, these people always take the apparent forms produced by the coming together of causal conditions as things that really exist and will last forever. They are in a fog, caught in their own wishful thinking, and they take their own interpretations and suppositions about things as the whole of reality, and their misunderstandings arise from this. In the end they often hurt themselves and hurt other people too.

When we have the empty illusory perceptions brought on by greedy cravings for forms, sounds, scents, flavors, touches, conceptualized things, this will produce various kinds of false thoughts and greedy desires. When our greedy desires get satisfied, we sink into that kind of empty, illusory, evanescent happiness and cannot pull ourselves out of it, and we mistake this feeling for good fortune. Unfortunately, desires are insatiable, and people who pursue desires often end up like people drinking salt water to relieve their thirst: the more they drink, the thirstier they get. For example, for a child who has never seen a toy, a little stone can make him very happy. But when he discovers that there are actually so many new and fascinating toys in the world, but that he cannot have them, he loses the simple happiness. What's more, even if he has one toy, soon he will be thinking about those that he does not have yet. The great majority of us are also this way. We cannot see clearly the true characteristic of the world, and we lose our yearning for the good, and we often enter into evil ways. After a while we become deluded, and we crave the myriad worldly forms, and our minds are dragged in by the colorful world, and we are running around everywhere in confusion. Our eyes see wondrous forms, our ears hear beautiful sounds, our tongues taste delicious flavors, our noses smell all kinds of fragrances, our bodies crave all kinds of beautiful wondrous touches, like the intimate kisses and embraces between lovers, and so on. From then on, following these always changing apparent forms, our thoughts in constant confusion, we gradually get farther and farther away from the true mind and the true characteristic, and more and more deluded and confused by the colorful world. The more we crave everything in the conventional world that cannot last, the more we crave everything in the world, and the more we are unable to see clearly the true characteristic of the world. As it is said, "From delusion comes craving, and based on craving, more delusion." We gradually become unable to extract ourselves from this, and so we fall into this evil cycle, revolving around pain and suffering.

Even more to be feared is that once we enter into this kind of evil cycle, we do not reflect on our own behavior, do not seek to make spiritual progress, do not distinguish right from wrong, and we only obey the voice of desire. We constantly use various pretexts to excuse our greed and anger, and we do many evil deeds. For example, you feel that you love someone very much, but one day she wants to break up with you, and you lose all feeling of love, and then begin to hate her: you hate her abandoning you, you hate her changing, and you even forget that you told her how much you loved her, and how much you hoped she would enjoy good fortune. You fabricate all kinds of rationalizations for yourself, including how detestable her behavior was, and how much you were hurt, and how she went back on what she had promised you, and so on. So then you feel you are justified in hating her, and so you hurt her and frighten her with loathsome bitter words, and you may even try to take revenge on her. Is this love? This is just hatred produced by desires not getting satisfied. It is something empty and illusory and impermanent, but when people are always under the control of these illusions, they do things that make their consciences uneasy. What is conscience? It is your true mind, the awareness that knows you have taken many stupid actions because you cling to the illusory as real. When you recognize the true mind, and you can preserve the true mind, and you reach the level where you do not waver, this is nirvana. When you do not clearly understand the true mind, and you are confused about the here and now, and confused about the external world, and always worried about external things, this is samsara. So many tragedies in the world, like murder, robbery, lewd behavior, and so on, are all because of people's ignorance and their indulgence in ignorance. Thus we say that the teaching of samsara, the cycle of revolving in the six planes of existence, really exists for most people. Because the basic substance of liberation is the mind's clear understanding, when your mind is limited to ignorance, there is no way for you to be liberated.

Do Not Fall into the Spider Web of Desire and Greed

Many people think that greed is something for greedy officials, and only greed for wealth can be called greed. But in fact it is not like this. When you come in contact with the external world, and you develop an inordinate liking for something, and want to have it and do not want to lose it, greedy thoughts are produced.

Buddhists say that "a human incarnation is precious." Humans belong to the three good planes of existence. Only when one has accumulated a lot of merit can one become a human, and obviously a human incarnation is important. When we have a human body, our minds and spirits have something to carry them. When we have a human body, we can carry out the directions of the spirit. When we have a human body, we can build value that time cannot destroy. Because of this, we must take good care of this body that is not easily attained, and preserve its health. But gradually, we forget that the spirit is the principal subject of life, and so we take the physical body as the whole of life. This is like looking on a limousine as the same as one's dignity. We do not understand that the limousine has its own lifespan, and it is the same for the physical body.

When we do not clearly understand this point, we are always indulging in various physical desires, and we become more and more lazy, more and more ignorant, and more and more greedy. We cannot hear the voice of the spirit, and we do not know that this is not the life we need. We just dimly feel that the depths of our inner minds seem to be hidden in a gigantic black hole. To fill this black hole, we are constantly stuffing things into our minds: work, meals, games, shopping. We don't dare to let ourselves stop, for fear that if we quiet down and stop, we will be swallowed up by a great void and sense of unease. We don't know where that giant whirlpool will take us. We fear the unknown, and we are afraid to think about it. We know that once we keep thinking about it, we will discover an enormous error, and realize that what we have spent our whole lives pursuing is not the thing we truly need. But we are still not prepared with the courage and wisdom to change. Because of this, our fear of thinking about it, and our expectations about the answer, we cannot help getting lost and madly running away. But if we are running away without direction, how can we remedy the labor pains of the spirit, and how can we bring happiness? If we compromise with the forest of thorns in the palace of delusion, how can we let ourselves get out of the endless dark night?

Some people do understand that suffering and uneasiness are

brought on by desire, but they are still willing to submit to the dictates of desires. Why? Because they accept the false as true, and cling to the illusory as real, and they feel that if they let go of desires, they would lose the many pleasures of being human. They do not understand that the result of letting go of desires is in fact the complete opposite of what they think it would be.

Let's take an example. You are disgusted by frogs, and disgusted by the sounds they make. When you are surrounded by frogs, you certainly will not be able to tolerate the harassment, and you will feel that the frogs are launching a noise attack at you. But for people who know the true mind, and have given up desires, it is exactly the opposite. In their minds there is no troublesome agitation, there is only a kind of heartfelt happiness. This is because, in their minds, the noises the frogs make are nature's words of love, the expression of the frogs' friendship, a free symphony. Regardless of whether they are listening to an expensive concert, or quietly listening to the voice of nature, they are in the same happy state. So you tell me: ultimately, is that reduced pleasure, or is it torment?

Do not be afraid of the true mind that is facing you, and do not be afraid to live under the direction of the true mind. When you perceive this world with the true mind, you will discover that although the world is not as simple as people wish it to be, it is not as complicated as you imagine. Fundamentally, everything is in your head, and nothing is more than a dream, an illusion, a bubble.

Is the glittering morning dew that was on the leaves still there? It has already been evaporated by the sunlight, and its existence is like an illusion. Do people still enjoy talking about the absurd things you did when you were young? Probably only you yourself remember them, and a couple of years from now even you will have forgotten them — they too will disappear like dreams.

Our lives are a giant illusion. When you understand this point, you will face everything in life calmly, and not differentiate things in terms of good and bad and liking and disliking. Do not give rise to the discriminating mind, and try to savor everything in life, and live tranquilly and happily. You may be like me, and find a way to create something of value that time will not destroy, and in the midst of empty illusion and impermanence, establish a relative permanence. Can we say that such a life is still not fortunate enough?

Furthermore, what is desire? Desire is a mirage in the desert. It is food in the eyes of a hungry ghost. Desires are incomparably empty and illusory, but they can light a poisonous flame in your mind, and make you so anxious you cannot sit still. Why do they have such a powerful influence on us? Because, when we accept the false as real, our minds are always full of greed.

But many people are unwilling to accept this point, as their knowledge of "greed" is very one-sided. They often think greed is something for greedy officials, and only greed for wealth can be called greed. But in fact, it is not like this. When you come in contact with the external world, and you develop an inordinate liking for something, and want to have it and do not want to lose it, greedy thoughts are produced. For example, you like to eat lychee, and you know that if you eat too much you will get sick, but you still cannot stop eating—this is greed. You like the feeling of having an affair, and though you clearly understand that this partner is not right for you, you still casually accept the partner's advances—this too is greed. Everything that happens in life can reflect a person's greed. It is precisely because some people have no way of resisting the enticing delusions of greedy desires that they go beyond the moral baseline and do immoral things. Thus it is said that "greed" is the source of all evils. People always assume that all they have to do is find the appropriate way to handle things, and then the things they care about will last forever. So all they think about is how to protect their own advantage, and they will not let go of anything—they are greedy for reputation, greedy for profit, greedy for wealth, greedy for sex, greedy for everything in the world. They madly pursue all this: the more they have, the more they cling to it, and the more they cling to it, the more desires they have, and so they descend into a cycle of evil. Then they are like bees who have fallen into a spider web, and no matter how they struggle, they are tangled up in it, and cannot seem to escape.

But there are people who think that desire is the original force that pushes people and societies to constantly make progress.

They think that if there were no desires, the progress of people and societies would all cease. I disagree. Why? Because progress that is motivated by selfish desire is brought about at the price of damaging what is beneficial for living beings. Technological progress that disregards social duty and lacks a loving heart often brings about great disasters that would be enough to obliterate the human race. Landslides, floods, tsunamis, nuclear accidents... How many people lose their lives in disasters brought on by mass greed? Isn't this nature sounding the alarm for the human race? If the price paid in blood is still unable to wake people up, then the future of humanity is something to worry about.

By the same principle, if one person takes his own desires as the motive for making progress, then all his actions will be for the sake of gaining greater profits, and he will not hesitate to hurt others to profit himself. If so, no matter how much he has, or what kind of position he has attained, none of it brings benefit to the world. What's more, when a person buries his conscience and harms other people, there will certainly be no way for him to live in peace, and even if he does not repent, he will feel a sense of guilt, and fear that he will not be able to hold onto those things he traded his conscience for. He may examine his conscience, he may pursue fame and fortune, he may enjoy life, but isn't this just to enable himself to live more happily? So then, if you lose calmness and tranquility, and are always living amidst anxiety and worry, what meaning do any of your actions have?

The Discriminating Mind Is the Source of Myriad Evils

All the vexations that people feel are produced because
they cling to the "self." All the conflicts among people
originate with the discriminating mind. This is because when
you have the discriminating mind, there is greedy desire, and
hatred, and ignorance, and from that there is war and murder
and degeneration. Then there is samsara, the cycling through
the six planes of existence.

All the vexations that people feel are produced because they cling to the "self." Clinging to and being attached to the self we call "self clinging." It means thinking that in this world there is some eternally unchanging "self." There is another word for "self clinging" — it is called "selfishness." This means being accustomed to taking the "self" as the standard, and measuring everything in the world in terms of the self, and taking all your energy and putting on defending "me" and "mine." For example, to protect their own interests, some people will sacrifice the interests of other people. Some people, to protect the interests of their own family, will steal from other families. Some people, to protect the interests of their own nation, will attack the interests of other nations. "self clinging" is the foundation for greedy desire. A person who clings to the "self" feels that everything is "mine" and that "I" am the main character in the world, and wants to take everything for "me" to use, and thinks that "my" feelings always matter the most.

Let's take an example. At one time the Japanese coveted China's vast territory and rich resources, so they launched a war against China, and killed and injured many Chinese people, and left many families with wounds that were impossible to heal. In the eyes of the Chinese, this of course was atrocious violence, but in the Japanese history books, it was painted over in colors of pathos and heroism. This is because, from the Japanese point of view, that war was launched for the economic security and survival of future generations, and it was also a product of patriotic fervor. Take another example. At one time Genghis Khan launched a war against foreign nations, and the land beneath the feet of his cavalry horses was soaked in blood, but in the eyes of people today, this kind of man was a hero of his time. Such a narrow moral viewpoint is very much to be feared, because to the people who uphold it, when there is a clash between what benefits "me" and what benefits "them," they will always sacrifice "them" to protect "me." What this "me" means is the self in people's minds, and it also includes the group closest to themselves, like my nation, my ethnic group, my city, my family, I myself, and so on. This is a strong kind of discriminating mind, and it is also dualistic. In this giant dualism, we take the "self" and clearly differentiate it from the external world. Almost all forms of cultivating wisdom are done in order to counteract the discriminating mind. This is because all the conflicts among people have their source in the discriminating mind. This is because when you have the discriminating mind, there is greedy desire, and hatred, and ignorance, and from that there is war and murder and degeneration. Then there is samsara, the cycling through the six planes of existence.

Nevertheless, many people do not clearly understand this point. They give free rein to the narrow moral viewpoint that is derived from this discriminating mind. It occupies the mainstream position in the world, and that is why all kinds of evil conflicts develop in every corner of the world, and relationships among people are becoming more and more estranged and cold. It is precisely because of this that all kinds of tragedies occur in every era, in every nation, in every family, every minute and every second. Something poisonous has been put into the food and drink; robbery, rape, murder, domestic violence increase like a swarm of mosquitos; swindlers make retired elderly people lose the few assets they need to care for themselves in their old age...

We all know that many dark things are hidden in society, and we all detest that darkness, but there are not many people who are willing to fuse with the subtle light of great good. People are even unaware that they themselves are a part of the darkness. This is because the great majority of people are too concerned with individual gain and loss, and too preoccupied with the "self" in their own minds. They rarely think about what kind of influence their own words and deeds are having on the external world, and just feel that everything is as it should be. But so-called good means that, at the same time as you are considering yourself, you should consider others more. Great good is more about letting go of your own expectations, and taking more consideration of others. If you cannot eliminate self clinging, then it will be very difficult for you to genuinely do this.

In reality, what is the "self?" It is a fabulous false semblance.

Our bodies are always changing, and because of our various experiences, our thoughts and habits are also constantly changing. We are already not that person we were yesterday, and we are not the person we were a second ago. We may have already grown tired of the things we liked last year, and we may even have grown tired of the people we used to love, and we may have grown tired of the styles of living we used to enjoy. Our points of view are even more like clouds in the sky, constantly changing shape.

A student told me that she once said to a boyfriend who was breaking up with her that she would wait for him for two years. Who knew that a year later the boyfriend would actually come looking for her, but her own feelings had already changed completely. When she thought of this, she always felt that she had done something foolish, and she felt ashamed. She did not understand that her foolishness was not in anything she had done, or anything she had said, but rather lay in not knowing that personal love is just an emotion, and the words that are said are just emotions. Even if she was sincere, words conveying some kind of emotion would always vanish the moment the words came out of her mouth, because emotions are constantly changing. Furthermore, foolish or intelligent, it was all something that had gone by. Once something goes by, it changes into a memory, and there is no need to be concerned with it. Many people cannot forget about things that have gone by, and cannot let go of their worries about the future, and so they live very painful lives.

In fact, clinging to your own foolishness and mistakes also happens because you feel that there is some eternal "I" in this world. Am I intelligent? Do the things I do satisfy other people? Do other people like me or not? Can I get more opportunities? Am I an excellent person or not? ... We are constantly sketching an empty illusory form, and taking it as a real genuine "self." We are always wanting to have other people understand this "self" and accept this "self." What's more, in order to get other people's approval, we are constantly adjusting our viewpoint, and we even do things that we are unwilling to do. Why? Because we are afraid of being lonely, and we need to be loved. Although there are some people who dare to reject the world, and they have the awareness and courage to think independently, they also fall into another fallacy — arrogance. They think that they are superior to other people, and they still cling to that "self" which seems so very real.

But this so-called "self" is just a product of the coming together of causal conditions, and like any individual link in the chain of causal conditions, it is constantly changing form: with more experience, your way of thinking will change, and your individuality will also change. When you eat more, you will put on weight, and when you do more exercise, you will get thinner again. People who can endure pain might go have a facelift… How can there be a "self" that does not change in the world?

Self clinging is like trash in your blood vessels. If this trash is not removed, it may form an obstruction in the blood vessels, and give a person all kind of uncomfortable sensations, so that affliction arises from this. After you clear away this trash, and restore the smooth circulation of the blood, the uncomfortable feeling dissolves away. By a similar principle, when you continuously clear away the filth in your mind and spirit, and gradually detach from the various clingings and attachments, and let your mind and spirit return to a state of purity and clarity, with no worries, then you will spontaneously be able to be liberated from all sorts of afflictions. Of course, this all begins with you recognizing the true mind, and discovering the true characteristic of the world.

Wake Up From the Delusions of False Thoughts

Many people live amidst the deceptions of false thoughts, but they are often totally unaware of this. They always think that the way they think about things is the reality of the facts, and so they use this so-called reality to put pressure on themselves, and seek afflictions for themselves. This is why the ancients said that there is basically nothing in the world, but people worry about troubles they imagine for themselves.

A friend told me an interesting story: One time she went with someone else to a pub to have a heart-to-heart talk. The two of them separately ordered bottles of sparkling water. There was no way she would drink alcohol, and so as soon as she had drunk half of the soda water, she began to feel dizzy. No one knew that someone else had taken her bottle of wine and looked at it and discovered that the alcohol content of that "wine" was zero. In other words, that friend of mine ended up becoming intoxicated by a half bottle of sparkling water. Later this episode was taken as proof that she could not drink alcohol, and this amused many people. But was what made her intoxicated really that bottle of sparkling water? Of course is wasn't. What made her intoxicated was a false thought that could take something false and confuse it with something real.

Many people live amidst the deceptions of false thoughts, but they are often totally unaware of this. They always think that the way they think about things is the reality of the facts, and so they use this so-called reality to put pressure on themselves, and seek afflictions for themselves. This is why the ancients said that there is basically nothing in the world, but people worry about troubles they imagine for themselves. Why do people always worry about troubles they imagine for themselves? It is because most people accept the false as true, and do not understand the true characteristic of the world. It is just like someone who is pursued by a wild animal in a dream, and falls into extreme fear. As soon as the person wakes up, and knows that it was only a dream, the person is set free from the empty illusory fear. Thus it is said: All we have to do is recognize the truth of impermanence, and stop clinging to the illusory as real, and then we will be able to escape from the deception and control of false thoughts.

The power of false thoughts is very strong. All our ways of thinking, all our attitudes, all our knowledge of the world is stained by the traces of false thoughts, because we have too many personal standpoints and biased views. Of course, sometimes these also originate from the social consensus accepted in common usage. But does the social consensus represent the true characteristic of the world? Obviously, it does not. We all know that there is an apparent form called the "collective unconscious."

In life there are many examples of the collective unconscious. For example, some people would rather take on the burden of a debt that will be difficult to repay, to buy a house. Some people are willing to get married only when they have bought a house. Some people feel that they are living for the sake of the house: as they see it, only their own house is really a home, and only when they have their own house will they have a feeling of security. Here's another example. Many people feel that doctors today take curing people as just a job, and many of them lack the slightest bit of compassion a medical practioner should have. But they still hope that their own children will be able to become doctors or marry doctors, because doctors' salaries are high, and their prospects are good, and being a doctor is a sign of social status...

A chaos of value systems is the most common demonstration of "collective unconscious" in contemporary society. Most people are accustomed to using many criteria—like wealth or social position—to interpret and evaluate themselves and other people. Their attention on topics like establishing businesses and getting rich goes far beyond their focus on wisdom and enlightenment. But they do not understand that if the foundation on which the edifice of life is built is not solid, the smallest setback can bring the whole building tumbling down. The suicides of many people who are socially prominent, or of film stars, are powerful proof. We can see that although false thoughts are formless, they can dissolve away reason, and cause people to descend into the false forms of pain and suffering to the point that they cannot extricate themselves or detach from them.

So then, how can you escape from the control of false thoughts, and return to the original pure true mind? First you must understand clearly what false thoughts are. False thoughts are thoughts born relative to objects, and they are constantly changing along with the changes in external objects. For example, you have never eaten durian, but you feel that it smells very bad, so you find durian very disgusting, to the point that you loathe waiting in the same room with a person who has eaten durian. But then one time a woman you like invites you to eat durian with her, and so you have no choice but to do it, and who would have known — once you try it, you get to like it. From this point, you not only do not feel disgusted by its odor, but you even come to like all food related to it. Therefore we say that our discriminating mind contains various likes and dislikes, and they are all built of false thoughts. When you abide in peace in the true mind, and you are not entangled in false thoughts, it is the wondrous functioning of the true mind, and it can help you perceive this world. But when you are entangled in false thoughts, and you let them continuously multiply like bullfrogs breeding, they will throw your mind into confusion, and render you incapable of finding the correct direction.

Let's take another example. You hear that a certain celebrity has donated a large sum to a charitable organization, and so you are full of good feelings for her. You even come to love all the films in which she has played a leading role. But later you also hear that her donations are just a hype, and your good feelings toward her are greatly discounted, and her films become insipid and dull. Then in the news magazines, you see her in tears trying to vindicate herself, and involuntarily you are filled with pity for her, and from this pity, your love is reborn... All these changes are based on what you have heard, what you have seen, what you have thought. Because of this, every time anything appears, it always influences how you see. Do these ways you see her truly represent herself? Of course not—these are only your false thoughts.

The world as it is in the mind of each person is always a manifestation of the person's mind and spirit. This is the reason why people who think of everything in terms of utilitarian gain have no way of understanding other people's unselfishness or philanthropic love, and greedy people always feel that their enemies are everywhere.

Many people feel that they are being controlled by the external world, but in fact it is not so. The reason you feel that you are being controlled is because you accept the false as true, and see everything as really existing, and so you give rise to a lot of desire and greed. If only you can adapt to conditions, be content, and abide in peace in the true mind, then the external world will not be able to disturb your tranquility and happiness. For example, if you do not seek anything from someone, then you do not have to look at the expression on his face to decide how to act—it is just this way. Obviously, after we have fulfilled the basic requirements for survival, the only thing that really binds us is our own habits, emotions, and biased views.

I will give you a simple example. There are three people in a desert. One is very negative and passive, one is very positive and active, and one is active but also adapts to circumstances. When these three people only have half a bottle of water left, the passive person feels terrified, and the active person feels satisfied because he still has half a bottle of water. The person who is active but also adapts to circumstances will value the water he has, but in a carefree yet alert way, he will look for a source of water. How does he know he will surely find a source of water? In reality, he does not know what might happen in the future, but he very clearly understands that there are many things he has no way of controlling. Therefore, he would rather enjoy the present moment, and he is unwilling to waste this precious life in endless false thoughts. He is only concerned with doing well the things he can do, and so he abides in peace in calmness and tranquility. He does not go off thinking about why he did not bring more water, he does not go off thinking about when he will be able to find a source of water, he does not go off thinking about whether or not he will die of thirst, and he does not focus on his terrible thirst. He is like the leading female character in my novel *The Spells of Xixia*: letting her mind go, she calls on the desert wind to blow away the dusty dregs in her mind, and she calls upon the blue sky to wash away the conventional sentiments from her spirit. How beautiful and wondrous this poetic sense is.

Human life is like this. You must not regret the past, and you must not be anxious about the future. All you can do is take hold of the present moment properly, and try your best to do those things you must do, and bring something beneficial to this world. As for the rest of it, just let it go. If you act this way, then you will spontaneously live this kind of poetic sense.

Doubt Is the Great Enemy of Happiness

People who like suspicion and doubt always give a utilitarian interpretation to the behavior of others. For example, when they see someone else encouraging good conduct, they think that the person must have ulterior motives he cannot tell people about. In fact, what the suspicious person sees is not the other person's motives, but rather his own suspicious mind. This is because the world as seen in each person's eyes, is the manifestation of the person's mind and spirit.

There was a young friend who told me that she was an extremely skeptical person, and that apart from her mother, she did not believe anyone, including her own husband. As soon as her husband was out of her sight, she worried that her spouse would go astray. Once she was away from home for many days, and the first thing she did when she returned home was to check the bed to see whether or not there were any other woman's hairs. Later she did indeed find a long curled hair, and so she took this hair and ran to interrogate her husband. As it turned out, it was actually her own hair—only then did she stop worrying about it. But her suspicions became hurtful for her husband.

Obviously, being suspicious is not a good habit, and it can bring people endless affliction. Moreover, people with many doubts will often harbor doubts about everything: they do not believe in other people's good intentions, they do not believe in love, and they do not believe that anything in this world is nobler than them. They certainly do not believe that there are unselfish people in this world who would rather sacrifice themselves and help others get what they need.

Once I heard some people talking about the "true characteristic" behind the good deeds of (the renowned Red Army soldier) Lei Feng. They said that if Lei Feng himself had not talked about it, other people would not have known what good deeds he did, and his joy in helping people was, in fact, nothing but glorifying himself. They also said that doing good deeds was the fixed standard for army men at that time, and he did what he did to win glory for himself. This talk made me feel very helpless. I felt that people who hold this point of view are even sadder than the point of view itself.

Why did they say such things? Why is a noble spirit no longer praised by people, but on the contrary, ridiculed, mocked and doubted? This no doubt reflects a kind of decline in human nature. People no longer believe in greatness or nobility. They no longer believe that there are people who can control their own desires, or who consider the benefit of others more important than their own. Why is this? It is because they must make their own greed and self-indulgence appear more rational, because they are looking for excuses for their own desires and selfishness. Their doubting and sneering in fact is an attempt to persuade themselves and suppress their own conscience and thirst for good. They are using this method that is not necessarily correct to soothe their own uneasy minds. Otherwise, how can they tell themselves why they cannot do the things that other people can do? Simply put, this is deceiving oneself and deceiving others. The majority of people, deep in their hearts, long for a world that is better than the present. But when some good news appears in society, they still like to use their so-called "rationality" and "realism" to dismiss it — how contradictory this is!

Sometimes, to protect themselves, people do not dare to believe other people easily. They continually torment themselves with suspicions and presumptions, and at the same time they are also tormenting other people. But they do not know that this is a kind of torment; on the contrary, they feel that only by doing this are they being shrewd and lucid. Thus, they not only harbor doubts toward people who are willing to help them, they also harbor doubts about the methods of liberation which their teachers teach them, and they even harbor doubts about themselves. By harboring doubts, they constantly harm themselves, and they harm other people who genuinely care about them. They cannot understand that the moment they harbor doubt, they shut out the other person's good intentions and helping hand.

People who like suspicion and doubt always give a utilitarian interpretation to the behavior of others. For example, when they see someone else encouraging good conduct, they think that the person must have ulterior motives he cannot tell people about. In fact, what the suspicious person sees is not the other person's motives, but rather his own suspicious mind. This is because the world as seen in each person's eyes is the manifestation of that person's mind and spirit.

When the majority of people use evil suspicions to dispel anything noble and well-intentioned, to wipe away any spirit of great virtue and great beauty, the society enters into what the Buddha spoke of as "the age of the end of the Dharma." This is because the human race at that time is already without faith, and has lost hope, and has abandoned itself to despair, and no longer thinks of turning toward the good: people go on harming others and harming themselves. Therefore we say that "doubt" is the great enemy of cultivation, and even more so, the great enemy of happiness. On the other hand, "faith" is "the mother of virtue." Only faith can enable people to actively advance upward, to go toward the good and avoid the evil. Only faith can let people build something of value that time cannot destroy.

However, though indiscriminate doubt is not good, indiscriminate faith is not good either. Both are manifestations of ignorance, and both lack the ability to tell right from wrong.

Completely indiscriminate faith is a deluded kind of faith, akin to superstition. People with deluded faith entrust liberation to things outside the mind. They think that their own liberation must depend on other people, or must depend on worshipping certain people or certain things, or worshipping this or that god or spirit. They completely fail to consider what they themselves must do, and act like slaves. Nowadays there are many people with deluded faith, and they do not understand that liberation is their own task.

Then too, when a person cannot understand how to tell right from wrong, there is no baseline for what the person should do. Because his "faith" is entirely a matter of following blindly, he cannot tell whether the person he believes in is actually a person of wisdom or a charlatan. If the person he has met is someone who genuinely conveys the truth, then his faith is a good thing, because he will be following a good man doing good things. But if the one he has met is just a charlatan who fabricates the truth for personal gain, then his faith is a disaster, because he will become the charlatan's accomplice, and unwittingly pass along those false theories. He may even slander people who are on a different path from him, and cause even more people to be deceived and harmed.

How do you distinguish people of wisdom from charlatans? You must observe their behavior. No matter how well a person talks, his behavior will always reveal his mind and spirit. If the truth he verbalizes cannot change his selfish, self-seeking mind, and cannot make him manifest the spirit of benefitting living beings in all his actions, then he is a charlatan. No matter what the rationalizations, they cannot conceal his selfishness — you must clearly understand this point. If the person you have faith in is a charlatan, then no matter what level your faith in him reaches, you can never be redeemed. On the contrary, you will fall to a lower level because of this blind faith. Thus it is said, we must detach ourselves from ignorance, and clearly distinguish right from wrong.

True faith must be the kind of faith based on wisdom.

Anger and Arrogance Are Stumbling Blocks for Freedom

When we cling to the false appearances of the self and to empty illusory gain and loss, we are sure to produce many expectations and illusions of the external world. When these expectations and illusions cannot be realized, we will feel a sense of loss, we will suffer pain, and various kinds of afflictions.

In a bustling city, you will often see this kind of scene: everyone is very busy, very rushed, and the slightest friction can call forth a volcanic eruption of hatred. Thus on buses and train you can often see quarrels provoked by people unintentionally bumping into each other. A student told me that she once saw murderous anger flare up because of slight contact — impelled by this, one man grabbed the other man by the throat. Obviously anger and hatred are demonic, and can incite people to lose their reason and do things that violate moral standards.

Anger is rage. A person who is raging is like a drunk — he has lost his reason. When you are burning fiercely with the flames of anger, you cannot feel love, and you cannot feel joy and happiness, and all sense of yearning for and upholding the good is incinerated by the anger and goes up in smoke. Imagine: if that man in a state of murderous anger had not calmed down in time, and instead had indulged his own anger, he might have actually killed the man who had gotten into a dispute with him. If he had really done that, then inevitably he would have had to bear the responsibility for his crime, and this responsibility would have been a reactive force of the world feeding back on him. The most direct form of the reactive force to angry behavior is losing all tranquility, happiness and calm, and falling into regret, guilt and anxiety.

What's more, when the flames of anger arise, the mind is no longer pure and clean. Then the empty spirit is no longer there, and wisdom is no longer there. All the pure clarity and wisdom in your mind is burned up completely by the flames of anger. Is this something the external world imposes on you, or something that originally belonged to you, but had been taken away by the external world? Remenber, it is your mind that clings to personal gain, that lets you descend into pain and suffering. In reality, the moment that incited you to anger has already passed.

Is someone unintentionally bumping into you enough to constitute a reason for killing the person? Obviously not. It is just a very minor detail of something that passes by in a moment like an illusion or a dream or a bubble, a minor memory. So why, because of this, did that man have a murderous impulse? Maybe it was because he had too much pent-up anger, and that had put his mind and spirit in a constant state of anxiety and depression. His hatred was like an inflated ball that had been forcibly held underwater, and the moment he forgot about it, the ball of anger fiercely shot up to surface, and created an unimaginable shock to his mind and spirit. At this moment he involuntarily gave rise to a murderous intent, and even the corresponding action.

There are many examples of this kind in society. If someone lacks a sense of accomplishment in life, he might harbor deep hatred, and release the fire of his anger on some group weaker than him. He may have frequent outbursts of anger, he may even abuse his wife, his children, or his pets. This is because, when he is venting his anger, his wife, his children, his pets are no longer objects of his love, but part of the external world — even if they are innocent. His behavior is continuously planting the seeds of evil, and when these seeds sprout and bear fruit, he will receive the karmic rewards of evil. Then again, when a person cannot help but release his anger on weaker, smaller living beings, he is in fact very pathetic. His pathetic quality lies in his ignorance, his weakness, his helplessness, and his hopelessness.

Why is it that people understand anger is not a good thing, and that it can make them impulsively do things that are utterly without benefit to themselves, and that it can damage their own health and emotional state, and that it can indirectly harm those around them, and yet they still cannot help having outbursts of anger, and even feel that their anger is justified? It is because they look upon everything as too real. In other words, this happens because they accept the false as true, and cling to the illusory as real. They do not know that the world is illusory transformation, that it is impermanent, that it is changing every minute, that everything is no more than a dreamlike memory, that the thing that made them angry has already passed. For example, some people hear someone else cursing at them, and they get very angry, because they feel that the other person has hurt their dignity. But genuine dignity is a kind of steadfastness within a person's mind — how could someone's words steal something from the person's mind? Therefore it is said that the true cause of someone getting angry is when another person makes him lose face. But what is this "face?" It is how other people view him, and other people's view of him, be it good or bad, is all a kind of emotion, a kind of memory, a kind of something that is constantly changing. If he wants to take this kind of impermanent thing and stabilize it in some state that is comparatively satisfying to him — like a person trying to grab water in his hand — he is doomed to fail.

When we cannot see through the many contradictions in life, and we cling to the false appearances of the self and to empty illusory gain and loss, we are sure to produce many expectations and illusions of the external world. When these expectations and illusions cannot be realized, we will feel a sense of loss, we will suffer pain, and various kinds of afflictions.

Clinging to the "self" sometimes can also make us arrogant.

Buddhism views arrogance as one of the barriers to the five virtues. This is because if you have arrogant views, you feel that you yourself are very wonderful, and other people are not good enough. Thus you generate many discriminating thoughts. Arrogance glorifies the self; it is not the same as "pride in our inherent enlightened essence." Pride in our inherent enlightened essence means recognizing that sentient beings are buddhas, and giving rise to a solid feeling that buddha and oneself are not two things, that what is mind is buddha, and advancing from this to solidify a detached mind of faith. But arrogance is not like this—it makes a person think that he himself is always right, and nobody else is good enough. He thinks he is stronger than everybody else, and if someone else begs to differ, he will then feel dissatisfied, and refuse to accept this. The mental state of such a person is terrible. Why? Because he will obstinately go his own way, and be headstrong and opinionated, and think that he alone is right, and everyone else is wrong. Then this person will not even be able to listen to the words of an enlightened teacher.

Keep Your Eyes Open, and Stay Far Away from Evil Companions

How do you tell the difference between evil companions and true spiritual teachers? A true spiritual teacher is a person who extinguishes afflictions like greed, ignorance, and hatred, and lets the love in your mind increase day by day. A true spiritual teacher can lead you toward happiness, freedom, and great good. The opposite of this is an evil companion.

We are always saying that all cultivating practice in life is for the sake of strengthening a person's inner mind. It enables us to see clearly and even dissolve away all the bad habits that produce afflictions and make us stray from the true, good and beautiful. But in reality, as long as the strength of our minds and spirits is not sufficient to resist the defilements of the external world, we must carefully make distinctions, and avoid the defilements of evil environments, and avoid being subject to the defilements of evil companions.

The defiling influences of environments of ignorance can

turn a child of humans into a wolf cub. The defiling influences of evil environments can make a conscientious person degenerate and turn toward evil. This is very much to be feared. But the effects of evil companions are no less dire than the effects of evil environments. This is especially true because some evil companions can assume the guise of good people, and pass along to you some specious "life wisdom." This will make you unwittingly susceptible to their misguided teaching, and gradually turn you into the kind of person you previously abhorred.

So then, how can we distinguish between evil companions and genuine spiritual teachers? A true spiritual teacher is a person who extinguishes afflictions like greed, ignorance, and hatred, and lets the love in your mind increase day by day. A true spiritual teacher can lead you toward happiness, freedom, and great good. The opposite of this is an evil companion.

Ultimately, how evil are evil companions? The classic teachers said that sometimes meeting an evil companion can make a person "not return for ten thousand eons." For example, after being on close terms with an evil companion, you may lose your faith, stray far from the correct path, and create great evil, or you may encounter difficulties in life, or lose you life. All of this is "not returning for ten thousand eons." In fact, many people who choose evil companions will experience in their lives the evil results brought on by such choices, and this is something very much to be feared.

I have seen many such examples. There was a young man who had always believed in Buddhism: his manner was modest and gentle, and he was very moral in his way of living and the way he did things. Later, unfortunately, he met an evil companion. Bewitched by him, the young man turned his back on his faith, and contaminated his whole life with defects: he played little tricks, he indulged in duplicity, being outwardly obedient but inwardly defiant, and he slandered the true faith. Later he left home and became a monk, but before long, he went back to the city. He would take off the monk's robe to chase women and play around, and then put the monk's robe back on and receive people's offerings. As he was at that time, he had obviously become degenerate.

Another example: There was a kind-hearted woman. Unfortunately she encountered an evil companion, and fell into his clutches, and they lived together for many years. First she became depressed, and later she contracted an incurable disease. Someone asked the physician treating her about the reason she had gotten this evil sickness, and the physician said: If you are trapped in a room with a wolf for several years, you will get cancer. He said that many diseases are brought on by depression. Before getting sick, many people who suffer from cancer have gone through a period of severe emotional distress. The physician added that if a white mouse is confined in a cat's cage for a long time, then the mouse may develop malignant tumors.

The material below was selected from a Baidu article on "Causes of Cancer:"

The factors that cause cancer are very complex, but spiritual factors have an important function in the origin and development of cancer. Contemporary medicine has discovered that cancer tends to develop in people who, after experiencing setbacks, have fallen into a state of spiritual depression, anxiety, dejection, anguish, fear, grief, and other such emotions. It is not that spiritual psychological factors can directly cause cancer, but that they often give a slow, continuous stimulus that influences and lowers the body's powers to ward off disease, and thus increases the probability of cancer developing. These stimuli function principally through the interrelationships of three systems: the biology of the nervous system, the internal secretions of the nerves, and the immune system. Ultimately they cause an increase in the secretions of ketone in the adrenal cortex, which enters the blood circulation, and thereby damages the body's ability to ward off sickness, and causes normal cells to become cancerous. Research reveals that when the stimulus of intense spiritual stress makes people lose the power to cope, and manifest the emotions of depression and grief, it can cause the excessive secretions of corticosteroid hormones, and thus depress the powers of the immune system. Then, when the immune system is suppressed, cancer may form. Specialists have also discovered that in people who are extremely depressed emotionally, the count of lymphocyte T-cells in the blood is conspicuously lowered, and the capacity to ward off disease declines.

In one research study, medical specialists discovered that 81.2% of cancer patients, before the onset of the disease, had undergone the impact of negative life experiences. Parallel studies of 398 cases of stomach cancer in big cities like Beijing and Shanghai revealed one common point, which was that all the victims of stomach cancer had frequently experienced situations of suppressed anger. From this, it is clear that spiritual factors that are not good can bring on the development of stomach cancer. At the same time, research in various regions had discovered that people who have a cheerful disposition and a healthy spirit do not easily get stomach cancer. In traditional Chinese medicine, they also recognize that an excess in the "seven feelings" can bring on stagnation of the vital energy and the blood, and thus give rise to cancer. They think that "the hundred illnesses are all born from the vital energy" and "the myriad sicknesses are all caused by the mind." Animal experiments too have proven that under continuous spiritual stress, animals' bodies may develop tumors.

We can put it this way: people whose mental situations are horrible, whose emotions are tense, who are depressed, who are melancholic, are prone to cancer, and cancer likes to wrap itself around these people. To prevent in advance the development of cancer, we must not only ward off all the factors that cause cancer, but also preserve a good state of mind and stable emotions, and preserve the health of body and mind.

In history, there have been many exceptionally beautiful women who unfortunately married "evil" men. Most of them passed their years in a state of depression, and died without being treated for it. Thus the ancients had a saying: "A beautiful woman tends to be unfortunate in life." It was even a common occurrence for them to be directly destroyed by evil men.

In my recent work *The Holy Monk and the Spirit Woman*, Khyungpo Naljor witnesses this kind of event, and says:

"These girls who are good at illusory thinking always mold cheaters and scoundrels into artists and religious practitioners in their minds. Cheaters do no work at all, and know nothing about growing crops, and they do not work to support themselves. These girls, so lovable and so pitiful, think that they will make a contribution to the arts or to faith, but they fundamentally do not know that they are using their youth, life and love to support a lazy cheater. They even take their partners' controlling them and possessing them as love and are intoxicated and soothed by such behavior. If one of them again encounters an irrational scoundrel, or that woman discovers that she is being deceived but cannot save herself, or if she discovers the real state of affairs and it makes her get depressed, then a deadly disease enfolds her, and she loses her health. Her entire life will be wasted. You look on hopelessly at these women, so filled with yearning, being pushed into the embrace of cheaters who use the label of 'faith' or 'love.' Your heart aches as if it is being sliced with a knife, but all you can say is that the situation is hopeless. You know that once their brains have been confused by the fine wine of 'faith' or 'love,' even their grandmas would not want them. Even if you go ahead and shout as loud as you can, there is no remedy for the situation. Wait until the true state of affairs becomes obvious, and the uncooked rice has been cooked, and her sons and daughters are at her knee, and the ebb and flow has entered her mind — only then will she be able to recognize for herself the sufferings of life, and swallow the bitter wine. If she chooses to get divorced, she is taking the bitter fruit of her life and throwing it to her pitiful children."

This world is full of this kind of regret. This regret also becomes the best footnote for a truth the Buddha discovered: "All defiled things involve suffering."

As for those who get confused by evil companions and lose their faith and do many evil things, they will descend into the state of "not returning (to a human incarnation) for ten thousand eons." According to the Buddhist explanation, that not only cuts off the life to wisdom for this lifetime, but also makes you subject to endless pain and suffering for many lifetimes because of ignorance.

Therefore, while the strength of your mind and spirit is not sufficient to resist external objects, you must keep your eyes open, and stay far away from evil companions. And you must not be corrupted by their evilness just because you want to save them.

Section Four:

Because of Wisdom, Life Changes

The Mind of Detachment Is Not a Temporary Emotion

Genuinely seeing through the red dusts of sensory experience means getting rid of your former blind infatuation with the world of the senses. When you are no longer blindly infatuated with everything in the world, a huge sense of being fed up with it will be produced in your mind, and you will feel that none of it has any great meaning, and then you will want to escape from this empty illusory unreal world. At this time, you will generate a great mind of detachment.

In the *Lotus Sutra* they tell a story: There was a wealthy man, and he possessed a large house, but this big house only had a single door. One day, the house caught fire, but the rich man's children kept playing games, totally unaware of the imminent danger to themselves. The rich man got alarmed, and called out to his children: "Come out quickly. Outside the house there is a sheep cart, a donkey cart, and an ox cart, and you can play with them!" Once the children heard that, they rushed out of the burning house as fast as they could.

What does this story mean? What it is saying is that, in the eyes of the children having fun while surrounded by the fire, playing games was all there was. Most of us are like these children, because in our eyes desire is all there is, and we do not know that the basic substance of enjoying pleasure is actually suffering. Some people know well how to make a living, how to get the things they want, like money, profit, reputation, social status, and so on, so they seldom encounter setbacks. Some people have great karmic rewards, and their luck is very good, and so they seldom meet with adversity. But it is precisely because it is like this, that these people will sink into delusion while enjoying pleasure, and be ignorant without knowing it themselves. They do not know that, in fact, human life is full of suffering. What kinds of suffering? Birth, old age, sickness, and death are very painful. Seeking things without getting them is very painful. Being often apart from loved ones is very painful. Being constantly together with people you loathe is very painful. It is also very painful when the poisonous fires of greed and hatred and ignorance and arrogance and jealousy engulf your mind and spirit. If people have not yet awakened, they will sooner or later taste these eight kinds of suffering. The sad thing is that some people, even if they become aware of suffering, are still not willing to be liberated from suffering. Why? Because they feel that human life must be like this, and they cannot see any other possibilities. They think that lasting happiness is pure nonsense. In order to lead such people toward enlightenment, the Buddha sometimes used ingenious methods—just as the rich man in the story used the prospect of new playthings to lure his children out of the burning house. First he attracted their attention, and then slowly he opened up their wisdom. This is what is meant by "First he lured them with desires, then he made them enter into the Buddha's wisdom."

People who discover the true characteristic of the world as constantly changing illusion are like children who see the conflagration around them: they are indeed frightened, but they cannot give up the games they like to play. That is to say, when you want to be liberated from suffering and realize what is really valuable, you will discover that human nature is all desire, and all the empty illusions of the world are enticing you. They are like ferocious beasts surrounding you, looking for an opportunity to devour you. What's more, what surrounds you on all sides is like a secret forest. You have absolutely placed yourself in a strange territory, and it is impossible to assess anything. But as your fear of the unknown slowly intensifies, the pull of desire fades away bit by bit. One day, the fierce flames of fear swallow up the whole world of desire, and everything gets burned away. The sky is filled with dust and smoke, and everywhere you see images of destruction and decay, a total mess devoid of signs of life. You can no longer feel the least bit of attraction, and you feel that nothing in the world has any meaning. At this time you have genuinely seen through the red dusts.

Genuinely seeing through the red dusts of sensory experience means getting rid of your former blind infatuation with the world of the senses. When you are no longer blindly infatuated with everything in the world, a huge sense of being fed up with it will be produced in your mind, and you will feel that none of it has any great meaning, and then you will want to escape from this empty illusory unreal world. At this time, you will generate a great mind of detachment.

But the mind of detachment is definitely not an emotional feeling. It is a mind of genuine detachment produced after getting a clear view of the ever-changing fundamental substance of things. Some people feel that they have become sick and tired of all the pursuit of glory and profit in the world of the senses, and they do not want to be involved in anything, but they cannot resist attractions and stimulations, so this feeling of aversion is only a temporary emotion. For example, many of my friends say that they will not invest in the stock market, but when they see other people making money by investing in stocks, they cannot hold back, and go invest anyway. They do not understand that whether stocks go up or go down has no real meaning. Even great wealth in the end will always be lost for various reasons. This is the truth expressed in the classical verse: "The great ones of old, where are they now? Their graves are a mass of briars. " Only when we have truly understood this point can we produce a solid, genuine mind of detachment.

A student of mine told me that he had worked for many years in an environment of people conniving against each other, and all the people around him did not hesitate to use methods that hurt others to benefit themselves. He too was like this, but as he pushed along day by day, he gradually discovered that this kind of life seemed utterly meaningless, and that he did not know what he was ultimately looking for. Everything he had once possessed seemed like bubbles that had burst, and sooner or later disappeared from his life, and it was even more like this with the happiness built upon these things. What's more, he discovered that because he had been lost in this game for such a long time, it was no longer possible for him to trust anyone, and he had even begun to be on guard with his spouse, and be suspicious and calculating toward her. He could not find any place that would let him take off his armor, and he lived every minute of every hour in solitude, feeling lost and in fear of the unknown. What was even more tragic was that, even though all those who took part in this game were like this, every one of them considered this pain and suffering to be inevitable, or blamed the external world for it. He had tried many methods to reduce this pain and suffering, but other than facing his own mind and spirit, none of these methods helped the situation. So he came to understand that unless a person dares to acknowledge his previous ignorance, doubt the whole entrenched system of thought and behavioral norms, and pursue wisdom and truth by a method that is not necessarily accepted by the conventional world, he will keep on suffering.

After you have clearly understood this point, you will gradually feel tired of everything, as if you no longer care about any of it. Elegant clothes and delicious food will no longer attract you, and titles like general manager and CEO will no longer attract you, and you will lose the desire to pursue fame and fortune. You will only want to get the wisdom of liberation, and establish something comparatively eternal in this empty illusory world. You will begin to inquire into your own mind, pursue your dreams, and seek the meaning of life. You will be willing to spend your whole spirit and life for the sake of this meaning. Even if there is no way of getting other people to understand you, it will not matter. Because of this, you will form a strong mind of detachment, and begin the search for the path that leads people to liberation. After this, you will begin to cultivate practice, and your mind will begin to struggle. We certainly have to struggle with and cast off this mind of suffering and affliction.

Because you have the mind of detachment, your desires will gradually dissolve away. Your eyes will observe all the forms, your ears will hear all the sounds, but you will not be greedy for them. Your nose will smell all the scents, your tongue will taste all the flavors, but you will not cling to them. All the information that is received by the sense organs will no longer disturb your mind, because your entire body and mind are seeking complete awakening. The objects of your greedy desires will change from pleasures to ways of going beyond the ordinary and entering into the holy. The objects of your anger will change from the external world, to your own clingings and attachments. You will clearly understand that everything is empty and illusory, but you try in vain to build something relatively eternal. The various kinds of clingings and attachments will all be softened by your firm mind, and slowly melt into the light of the true mind. And you, yearning for the light, will finally gain an unconditional happiness.

The Enlightened Teacher Is a Beacon for the Spirit

The one who lets you become more pure, more expansive, more clear—this is the enlightened teacher. This is because the enlightened teacher can lead you higher, dissolve away your clingings and attachments, and give a wakeup call to the inherent wisdom of your inner mind. Someone who lets you get more greedy and more hateful and more deluded is an evil companion. This is because he can lure you down to a lower state, and offer you excuses for letting yourself go, and incite you to do evil deeds to protect his own gain, and increase the negative powers of your inner mind.

No matter by what method you hope to strengthen your mind and spirit, you always need a good teacher. This good teacher might be a truly enlightened person of wisdom; it might be something big or small in life; it might be a good book; it might be a special experience, and so on. Of course I myself particularly recommend meditation. Over a thousand years, a great deal of experience has been accumulated in cultivating meditation buddhas, and it is the summation of various methods that are effective when carried out, methods that match the particular needs of various kinds of people. Therefore, I think that finding a genuine teacher, taking refuge with him or her, and cultivating your mind and spirit under his or her direction will save you a lot of time fumbling around on your own, and will help you avoid the detours and pitfalls on the road.

Of course, someone who is called a "good teacher" must be an enlightened teacher. "Enlightened" here means having clear understanding and wisdom. This means that a genuine enlightened teacher must be a person who has genuine enlightenment and who possesses wisdom. In Buddhism they call this kind of person an "enlightened teacher." He or she is not necessarily famous. This is because among the people who are very famous, there are some charlatans without learning or practical abilities. A true teacher is not necessarily a monk or nun, because a person wearing clerical robes can be filled with greed, anger and ignorance.

After finding this kind of teacher, why is it necessary to take refuge with him or her? The term "take refuge" means to rely on someone. After taking refuge with an enlightened teacher, your mind and spirit will have something to rely on. This implies that you are willing to take your body, mouth, and mind and offer them to the spirit of great good and great beauty and great truth, and after this, all your actions and words and thoughts will be a vehicle for the spirit of great good.

When you are not yet enlightened, how can you be sure that

the one you have found is a genuine enlightened teacher? You must carefully observe your own mind and spirit. When you are in contact with the teacher, you must observe whether you are gradually becoming more pure and more expansive and more clear, or whether you are becoming more greedy and more angry and more deluded. The one who lets you become more pure, more expansive, more clear—this is the enlightened teacher. This is because the enlightened teacher can lead you higher, dissolve away your clingings and attachments, and give a wakeup call to the inherent wisdom of your inner mind. Someone who lets you become more greedy and more hateful and more deluded is an evil companion. This is because he can lure you down to a lower state, and offer you excuses for letting yourself go, and incite you to do evil deeds to protect his own gain, and increase the negative powers of your inner mind. If the other person is a genuine enlightened teacher, you must cultivate your mind and spirit well according to the methods he has taught you. If the other person is an evil companion, you must get away from him as quickly as you can, and block the various temptations and distractions he causes you.

Let's take an example. Some people, although they do not have the strength to escape from the bonds of desire, still know there are things that must be done and things that must not be done. But after they mistakenly come to have faith in an evil companion, the evil companion tells them, "You must struggle for greater gains, because only by doing this will you have the power to create benefits for society. Pay no attention in the early stages whether or not that struggle for gain will injure others: as long as you do not do these things *in order to* hurt other people, it is alright. You must cast aside all relative concepts of good and evil." If they believe what the evil companion says, they will pursue their desires under various pretexts, and protect their own profits, and for this they will not shy away from lying all the time, doing evil things and hurting other people.

You must know that a person's mind and spirit is like a wooden table: it is easily stained with grease. If you not only do not wipe it off, but constantly rub dirt into it, as time goes by, this dirt will penetrate deeply into the table, and become a part of the table. When the time comes that you want to wipe it clean again, it will not be that easy to do. What is more likely to happen is that, because there is no way to wipe that filthy table clean no matter how you try, you will just get rid of it once and for all. This means that if a person wants to sink to a lower level, it is very easy, and if he indulges himself, and does not remove the filth from his mind and spirit using appropriate methods, then he will rapidly degenerate. Unless he sincerely repents, resists the inner mind's evil power with strong faith and appropriate actions, and dissolves away the evil that was growing stronger day by day through his previous self-indulgence, it is very likely that he will ultimately end up becoming the victim of his own evil deeds.

Besides observing your own changes, you can also observe the other person's character. You must especially observe how that person handles conflicts of interest with other people. If a person does not hesitate to hurt others to protect himself, then he is absolutely not a teacher who can lead you to a higher level. This has no connection to whether or not what he says is reasonable. A genuine guide for the mind and spirit will not necessarily be a good talker, and will not necessarily have a benign look. Some teachers may even constantly scold you, scold you till you break out in a cold sweat. But if at the same time, you still feel that you seem to be understanding something because of this, they too are "enlightened teachers" Milarepa's master teacher Marpa often hit and scolded Milarepa, but Marpa was still a very enlightened teacher.

Sometimes, the sufferings and difficulties in life can become your teacher. For example, many people become grief stricken when family members or friends pass away, and they lose their attachment to the world of the senses, and give rise to a great mind of detachment. At this point they discover that many of the things they used to be attached to and pursue — salaries, material benefits, external appearance, enjoyment of material things, approval from other people, and so on — in fact basically have no meaning. Faced with impermanence, they collapse at the first blow, and fade away in the blink of an eye. For these people, family members and friends departing from the world is a disaster, but it is also a cooperating causal factor (in the process of spiritual learning).

Here's another example. Someone is very wealthy, but suddenly he comes down with an incurable disease, and the doctors tell him that no matter how much money he spends, there is no cure. At last he has a sudden realization that for many years he has been wasting his mind, and he tastes the full bitterness: the vast wealth he has accumulated by fair means or foul is in fact not worth a penny. So then he donates all his money to people in need. For this man, isn't it true that the incurable disease is an excellent teacher?

A further example. There is a man who has a wife, children, a car, real estate and money. Suddenly, in a financial crisis, he goes bankrupt. His car and his house are repossessed, and his children and his wife leave him. One day he is eating simple porridge, and he begins to think of his formerly prosperous life, and he feels that worldly things are like a dream, without the slightest feeling of being real. In his mind he becomes indifferent to them, and he lets go of everything, and from then on his life is really raised to a higher level. For this man, the financial crisis is an enlightened teacher.

In the inner mind of one person, great suffering can stimulate the most beautiful things, and in the inner mind of another person it can stimulate the ugliest things. The difference is a matter of whether you choose in the midst of suffering to sink into self-indulgence, or whether you wake up and go toward a higher level. Obviously, it is a fortunate person who can understand the truth that "adverse conditions are favorable conditions, and affliction is enlightenment."

When you generate an enormous mind of detachment, and you find an enlightened teacher who can lead you to a higher level, you still need a clear, true aspiration. What is called "generating aspiration" means making a vow. That aspiration is the goal that you must reach in this lifetime, the goal and orientation of all your choices and actions. In (the classic sixteenth century Chinese novel about the quest for wisdom) *The Journey to the West*, the aspiration of the White Dragon Horse is this: "I certainly must carry the Tang Monk to India to get the scriptures." Since he has this aspiration, his journey has a goal and a meaning, and thus he is able to proceed onward step by step, steadfastly, without slacking off. But the donkey in the mill has no aspirations, and though too he walks on day after day, his journey has no goals whatsoever, and he is just wasting his own life.

Generating the aspiration corresponds to the first of the three types of the people with great achievement in ancient times, which Wang Guowei (1877–1927) described: "Last night as the green trees withered in the west wind, he climbed the high tower alone, and beheld the road that goes all the way to the horizon." He beheld the road that goes all the way to the horizon, and then he generated the aspiration, and ultimately he decided to travel that road to the horizon. Without generating the aspiration, you cannot have the subsequent action.

Let Good Actions Change Your Mind and Spirit

When we take wisdom and pass it on, many people will understand the true characteristic of the world, and have wisdom, and become happy. After they have received the benefits, they too will take this wisdom of liberation and again pass it on. After we use the torch of wisdom to light the tinder in other people's minds, their minds also will become torches, and they will go on and light up the minds and spirits of more people.

After you have the mind of detachment, and you have found an enlightened teacher, you will then have the possibility of changing your mind and spirit. But whether or not the possibility can be brought to realization still depends on your own actions. You can start first by loving your own family members, and then take this love and propagate it bit by bit, and let it spread to more people, even strangers. When you have within you an unselfish love for other people, you will spontaneously do all you can to enable them to be blessed and happy. Then you will gradually learn how to contribute, and how to benefit living beings. Besides this, you can also do things according to Buddhist methods, like preparing fields of merit, and fostering the bodhi mind, and serving sentient beings.

What is meant by "fields of merit?" Fields of merit are your virtuous deeds and your meritorious virtues. The process of accumulating virtuous deeds and meritorious virtues is called preparing fields of merit. In general there are two methods of preparing fields of merit: the first is offering support, and the second is giving charity. Giving charity includes giving wealth, giving the teaching, and giving fearlessness. Of course there is also action in the category of releasing living beings: releasing living beings belongs to the category of giving charity, giving life.

What is called giving wealth is not only not taking other people's wealth, but also taking one's own food, clothing, property, jewels, money and so on, and giving it to other people. When you take your wealth to offer support to other people, this activity itself can create a kind of reactive force, and bring you great merit.

People who are unwilling to give charity are very ignorant. Their lives are filled with "me" "my" and "mine." They basically cannot see anything else. They do not know that while they are busy enjoying pleasures and pursuing wealth, there are many families who are falling into extreme misery, who do not have enough to eat, and who are even losing their lives. When they have absolutely no feeling for the sufferings of other people, their existence has no meaning whatsoever. Thus it is said that people who are unwilling to give charity are not anything. They do not want to throw away even the three coins they are grasping in their hands, but in the end they will lose them. High-ranking people all through history in all countries — when they are approaching the end, aren't they just like the destitute people, and won't they end up in coffins?

Moreover, experts think that the greatest secret in the world for making money is not to seek it, but rather to give charity. According to what they say, when you have the intention to give charity, and you act on this, your mind merges into one with a certain great force in the universe, like a little river flowing into a great ocean, and becomes a part of the ocean, and thereby gets the help of this great force, so you can then achieve your aspiration, and get the corresponding reward for merit.

An article called "The Greatest Secret in History for Earning Money" says the following:

"If a person consistently serves the interests of other people, to the point that this sort of good behavior becomes an unconscious habit for him, then all the good power in the universe gathers behind him, and he succeeds in his work. This is because, other than giving charity, there is no voice that can communicate as clearly to the universe your self-confidence, your abundance, and your love.

"And when the universe hears this, even more beauty and

goodness will be endowed to you — this is because you truly believe in your own abundance and love.

"When you give time, you will harvest time. When you donate goods, you will harvest goods. When you donate love, you will harvest love. When you donate money, you will harvest money.

"All prosperous people will give charity, some say, but I'd rather say all people who give charity will become prosperous."

Thus, giving charity is the greatest form of merit in the world, the greatest form of good conduct, and the greatest secret for earning money. It is like planting seeds in the ground: we must take the seeds and plant them in the fields, and only then can they flower and bear fruit.

But giving wealth is not the most important thing. Among all forms of giving charity, the most important is giving the teaching, giving the Dharma. Giving the teaching means that when you have gotten to hear the worldly truth and the world-transcending truth from the buddhas, the enlightened teachers, or the scriptures, and you have benefitted from this, you must then take the truth you have come to know, and transmit it to others with no thought of reward.

Giving the teaching is also a kind of activity that benefits oneself and others. Shakyamuni Buddha said that if you offer all the jewels filling all the worlds in the universe to support all the Tathagatas of the past, present, and future, the merit of this is less than the merit of transmitting the wisdom in the *Diamond Sutra* to one worldly person. This explains that "giving the teaching is superior to giving wealth." Because giving wealth can only resolve some of the recipient's temporary needs, but giving the teaching can create the possibility of changing someone's life forever, and can be passed along. Moreover, giving the teaching is more precious than giving wealth.

When we take wisdom and pass it on, many people will understand the true characteristic of the world, and have wisdom, and become happy. After they have received the benefits, they too will take this wisdom of liberation and again pass it on. After we use the torch of wisdom to light the tinder in other people's mind, their minds also will become torches, and they will go on and light up the minds and spirits of more people.

Thus, a person who genuinely gives the teaching must have the enlightened mind of benefitting sentient beings. The enlightened mind, the bodhi mind, is the pure mind that has no seeking. After you have the enlightened mind, you still have to express it by means of actions that benefit sentient beings. In the sutras, they take all forms of good action and sum them up into ten categories:

1. Not only do you not kill living beings, you also must carry out good deeds to set them free. You must do everything in your power to respect and help all living things, and let them exercise their right to live and survive.

2. Not only do you not steal other people's wealth, you must

practice the virtue of giving charity.

3. You do not give free rein to your emotions, and you do not engage in illicit lust; rather, you must purify your intent, and make energetic progress cultivating practice.

4. You do not lie or deceive, and you must treat other people with genuine sincerity and honesty.

5. You do not talk about who is right and who is wrong, much less foment discord. You do all you can to reconcile the contradictions among other people.

6. You do not speak evil, or slander other people, and you must use a calm, gentle manner when you converse with people.

7. You do not indulge in loose talk, and you do not flatter other people. You must be sincere and frank in your dealings with other people.

8. You are not to be greedy for emotional pleasures, and you do not indulge in emotional pleasures. You must purify your intent, and make energetic progress cultivating practice.

9. You do not engage in outbursts of anger toward other people, or bear grudges against them. You must treat other people with compassion and forbearance.

10. You do not give rise to biased, misguided, deviant views, and you do not cling to wrong as right. You must constantly focus on true faith and true perception.

The whole meaning of the Buddhist teaching is established on these ten kinds of virtuous action. They are in the category of a fundamental moral standard. Even more important, they can help you purify the defilements of the body, mouth, and mind, and enable you to keep away from evil environments. They offer cooperating causal conditions for your liberation. This is also the meaning of a code of conduct, of discipline. When you have gotten far away from evil, and you are going toward the path of goodness, and you are fully equipped with these ten forms of good conduct, you will be equipped with the foundation for achieving the mind that has no seeking. But if you want to benefit living beings, you still have to generate a dignified manner.

Dignity is similar to having confidence in your inherent enlightened nature; it is the genuine manifestation of your own inherent mind, and not some superficial false performance. True dignity is an attitude that is born in the pure mind after rigorously preserving discipline, an attitude that makes people feel respect and awe. It is the outpouring of the true mind. What it shows is a kind of deep faith in the truth, free of doubts, and a strong power to exert control over the body and mind. From the deep respect you feel towards this dignity, come faith and yearning for the truth.

A thousand years ago, Milarepa practiced austerities for many years in the mountain valleys, and was too busy to be concerned with food, drink, clothing and his outward appearance. He kept on practicing until he was emaciated, and his body turned green, and there were thick calluses all over his buttocks. But in the end he plucked the fruit of ultimate enlightenment, and only then did he begin to spread the teaching. This was the basic cause. Thus it is said, when you discard your set views and useless speculations, and enter into the inner minds of the people who genuinely cultivate practice, and experience their pure aspirations, and think back on all the efforts they made to seek faith, you will genuinely be moved.

True Maturity Is the Maturity of the Mind and Spirit

For the whole society, the whole human race, the whole world, is it or is it not better that you have been here? If you have not been able to do this, then you have not brought about anything of genuine value. What we call something of genuine value is the spirit of benefitting living beings. It is only when you have done things which genuinely benefit living beings that you have been able to bring about something of genuine value from the standpoint of the whole universe and all living beings.

What we call bringing the mind and spirit to full maturity is enabling your own mind to become more and more broad and profound. One day, when you are no longer calculating individual gains and losses, and you are unconditionally concerned for other people, you will achieve realization of what in Buddhism is called "unconditional great compassion, the great mercy of sharing the same essence with all beings." Then you will change from an ant into an elephant.

While you are still an ant, it may be hard for you to understand the mind of an elephant. You may not yet be able to understand what genuine maturity represents. You may think that your aim in life is to be constantly at your parents' side, and to provide your children with an excellent environment to live in. But do you understand what they need? Are you able to help them get the things they truly need? Probably not. This is because, before you have matured into an elephant, there is no way for you to correctly interpret their minds, and you cannot correctly interpret yourself either.

In everything that humans pursue, the goal is happiness. No matter what they do, it is always to get happiness. Painters paint, actors act, writers write, children frolic at the seashore — it's all to get happiness. Cars, buildings, money — all this appears because humans want to get happiness. But true happiness is too simple, too plain, and so many people overlook it, and instead go to the external world seeking something that is more like "happiness." This is like you seeking your mind in the world outside your mind — you will never find it. If you cannot find the thing you need, how can you give it to the people you love?

The maturity you need is not just the maturity at the level of survival skills, but a more fundamental maturity — the maturity of the mind and spirit. When your mind and spirit are strong enough, you will have a lucid clarity and self-confidence — "everyone in the crowd is drunk, but I alone am sober."

Then you will discover that no matter how much money you

make, how many fans you have, how many people know your name, none of this has any real meaning. Except for something with special merit, it all decays faster than the body. Generation after generation, people die, and who remembers what companies they worked for? Who remembers if they were managers or ordinary employees? Who remembers what make of car they drove? Who remembers how large their apartments were? No one. Your existence is like a fly streaking through empty space: it cannot leave any traces. This is because you have not created anything of value that will not be destroyed by time. That thing of value is what Buddhism calls merit.

Perhaps you have earned a lot of money for your company, and you have provided your family with great comfort, but the only ones you have benefitted are the people who are very closely connected to you. But for the whole society, the whole human race, the whole world, is it or is it not better that you have been here? If you have not been able to do this, then you have not brought about anything of genuine value. What we call something of genuine value is the spirit of benefitting living beings. It is only when you have done things which genuinely benefit living beings that you have been able to bring about something of genuine value from the standpoint of the whole universe and all living beings. This kind of value can get free of the bonds of the physical body, and be passed down from generation to generation, lighting the torch of wisdom in people's minds, and becoming beneficial nourishment for the human race. Shakyamuni Buddha was like this: his physical body disappeared more than two thousand years ago, but his wisdom still illuminates the human spirit today. This is a life with true meaning.

When I was ten years old, I saw death with my own eyes, and from that point on, I thought about death and feared it, and so it was always with me. I was always afraid that death would take away all evidence of my life, and at that point, what would be the difference if I had not lived? So I began to inquire into the meaning of being alive. Later the Buddha's spirit of feeding the birds and beasts with his own flesh illuminated my mind and spirit, and I finally understood what a person is ultimately living for, and what meaning being alive ultimately has. This meaning later became my standard for measuring everything: is your being in the world better than your not being in the world? It is also like this with my writings. I do not want to waste my precious time alive writing things I see as trash. What am I calling trash? If they cannot do the world a bit of good, if they waste my time and waste the readers' time—they are trash. My not being willing to write this kind of thing is not being aloof; rather, it is a choice. When facing the world, each person must lucidly make his or her own choice.

But what is too bad is that the majority of people do not know that they must do this, nor do they know they can do this. They live every hour and every minute as slaves to the external world. Intelligent people are especially this way—they do too much mental calculation, and understand too well how to juggle ideas. They fill their lives with totally meaningless things, and are reluctant to use even a little bit of time to focus on their own internal minds. They are too exclusively focused on profitable games. I know that they are the same as people in my hometown, who all feel that "death is like a candle going out, and once you die, there is nothing there anymore." This point of view is accepted by materialists. Those people who fear that after death "there is nothing there anymore" take advantage of any power and position they have to plunder wantonly, and thus there are so many greedy officials harming society. Materialists do not know that the point of view they champion is precisely the foundation for many people's unrestrained false behavior.

But Buddhists do not think this way. Buddhists believe in cycling through six planes of existence, and believe that the long river of life keeps flowing on without stopping. According to the Buddhist teaching, the human plane belongs among the three good planes of existence, and one can only be a human after accumulating the appropriate merit. Obviously the time a human is alive is very precious. If you waste it, you are in effect wasting lifetimes of your own painstaking efforts.

For the majority of people, they only become conscious of how short life is when they are approaching death. Originally we think that several decades will be enough time for us to do whatever, but in the blink of an eye, our hair turns white and our bodies stoop with age. Then we finally discover that our lives have just been an approach to death. Ultimately, what meaning does this kind of life have? In a television show, an older guy over fifty tells his son, "Your papa has lived his life without any dreams, and his whole lifetime has gone by in a flash." So many people are this way. But they do not know that they could have had another way of living. What way of living? Seeing through the dreamlike illusory quality of this world, and taking hold of the present moment, and doing things that have meaning for the world, and creating something of value that time cannot destroy.

When you have clearly understood this point, you will understand that all enjoyments are only empty false emotions and memories that will disappear in the blink of an eye. When you are indulging in them, you will forget your dreams, and forget the plain and simple happiness. You will let the flames of those desires constantly lick at your mind. In fact, no matter how other people evaluate them, these are all empty illusory impermanent things. Even if they can bring you pleasure or pain, they are only manifestations of your own mind. All the complex apparent phenomena and realms of experience in the world are reflections and manifestations of your true mind. They are all generated by your inherently empty, still and clear "mind essence." When our mind essence generates wondrous functioning, then, according to circumstances, it reflects two kinds of manifested objects, "defiled" and "pure." The "defiled" ones are the various kinds of realms manifested by the false mind. The pure ones are the various kinds of realms manifested by the undefiled true mind. When you understand this point, and see the true mind of inherent nature, you will also understand the true characteristic of the world.

Your clear understanding will illuminate the course of your life, and point out your direction. Then you will go on like this step by step, and keep going with steadfast assurance. The day will come when your mind's capacity gets big enough to be able to encompass the whole world, and transform everything in the world into nutrients for your mind and spirit. It will let your mind mature into a solid unbreakable great tree, with beautiful flowers blooming from its branches, and warming the whole world with its fragrance. At this point you at last truly mature from a child into an adult who can be autonomous.

The Object of Cultivation Must Be Your Mind

No matter what form of cultivation we use, its object must be our own mind. When the mind is corrected, in our actions we will naturally benefit living beings and go toward the good. That's why it is said that a straightforward mind is the place where the path is cultivated. When the mind begins to go astray, and be controlled by desires, people become an army of demons, and their behavior tends toward injuring others to benefit themselves.

Many people feel that cultivating practice is very difficult. What they especially cannot understand is that they are using methods that other people do not understand much about, like having a vegetarian diet, or meditating, to resist the desires inherent in human nature. But for those who truly have faith in Buddhism, these practices are not painful. Moreover, they are going toward the good is not because they fear "cycling in the six planes of existence" and "karmic retribution." For them, cycling through birth and death and the workings of cause and effect are simple facts, the same as the fact that smoking damages one's health; they are not moribund religion doctrines that bind the mind and spirit.

What is being sought by those who genuinely cultivate practice is an unconditional freedom, and all that they do is to break through all that binds the mind and spirit, and realize a total independence. So it is said that of course they are not looking for another kind of suit and tie and footwear. All those things in cultivating practice, which at first glance seem like forms of bondage, are no more than methods. They are tools to help practitioners distance themselves from evil defilements and purify their own intent. They are barriers to block the evil wind and rain from the external world. Before wisdom awakens, or, when wisdom has awakened, but the power of meditative concentration is insufficient, people cultivating practice still need to rely on the power of discipline, to restrain their actions tinged by desire, and to preserve the spark of enlightenment in their minds. When they can be awake at all times, and preserve their awareness of the true mind, they will no longer care about all the illusory causes and conditions in the external world. At that point they will not feel any sense of loss, because there is no way for them to have anything. This is because if they are fully equipped with ultimate wisdom, and they can use wisdom to observe the world, and they discover its empty illusory unreal quality, then they will no longer be deluded by it, and they will have achieved liberation. At the same time that they have this level of perception, all doubts and confusion are removed, and when doubts and confusion are removed, they will not be bound by them—this is the liberation that is sought by cultivating practice.

After you understand this point, and you take another look at the colorful world, you will become aware of how monotonous it is, and you will have sincere sympathy for the people who have become so besotted with it that they forget to return home. You will surely understand that this is another way of living, and this way of living has the sense of ease and satisfaction that they want, and you respect them. It may even happen that a person who is immersed in worldly pleasure wants to take his happiness and add it to yours, and you feel gratitude toward him. This is because you know that he is like a child who feels that sweet fruit is good to eat, and wants to let his parents have a taste. The parents know what the child has in mind, and he wholeheartedly enjoys this happiness which his thoughts have given him, but if he is not indulging in it, he will not demand it anymore. This is because indulging in worldly pleasures that are empty and illusory and impermanent is something that brings suffering. For example, when a certain toy is close at hand, but the child cannot get it, he will moan and cry, and even roll around on the floor—he is truly suffering. He feels that once he has this toy, he will be ten times happier than he is now. He does not know that he will soon get bored with this toy, and he does not know that sooner or later the toy will break — he only knows that he wants to get it. You understand the child's pain, but you do not necessarily have to indulge his desires. What is most important is that you, who are no longer a child, do not join in struggling with children over toys.

Apartment buildings, cars, money, all these things are in fact toys for adults. Children focus their attention on toys, and continually raise their own demands for toys based on what they have seen and heard, and we are the same way. But we are even greedier than they are, because the "toys" in our minds are more numerous, and the temptations are greater. These toys are our desires.

When you discover that everything in this world is a false form, an empty illusion, impermanent, without inherent nature, this level of perception can liberate you. At this time, you must change the way you refine your mind and spirit. This is because, when your mind and spirit have changed states, the methods and guidelines from before will turn into another kind of barrier, and you must sweep them out of your mind. But if you get a little bit of attainment and then feel that you have already entered a certain state, and you must transcend all names and forms, including the guidelines for cultivating practice, and distinctions between good and evil, and correct perception and so on, despite what you may think, there is no benefit in this. This is because you still cannot be certain that you have really escaped from the control of desires. Having no distinctions is not the same for the ordinary person as for the person of wisdom. This is because, for the former, it means taking the idea of truth as his own liberation, while for the latter, it is the manifestation of wisdom. However, no matter what form of cultivation we use, its object must be our own mind, and not the body, and especially not something like a feeling or a magical power. When the mind is set straight, our actions will naturally benefit living beings and go toward the good. That's why it is said that a straightforward mind is the place where the path is cultivated. When the mind begins to go astray, and is controlled by desires, people become an army of demons, and their behavior tends toward injuring others to benefit themselves. Those whom we speak of as evil demons and those outside the Path are those being led along by misguided minds.

In (the classic sixteenth century Chinese novel) *The Journey to the West*, the reason the Tang Monk became the Tang Monk was not because his flesh was delicious, but because his mind was correct. Because his mental state was correct, he was called "the Sage Monk." If his mind had been misguided, he would have been an evil demon. The reason Sun Wukong became a great sage, and in the end became "The Victorious Buddha," was because day by day his mind eliminated its ignorance, afflictions and scattering, and finally realized peace and tranquility. That is why it is said that the mind is the seed of cycling through birth and death, and the six planes of existence are created by this mind.

The Buddha said: "Do not commit any evil deeds, and

faithfully carry out all forms of good—this is the teaching of all the buddhas." Here he is requiring us to keep away from all evils, and to faithfully carry out all forms of good, and to use good thoughts to purify our own minds. When a person has not yet become enlightened, "Do not commit any evil deeds, and faithfully carry out all forms of good" is a standard for how to behave. After a person gets enlightened, it becomes a spontaneous natural result. The distinction here lies in the condition of the person's mind.

When you have not yet become enlightened, and you still accept the false as true, you always look upon everything as real. You care about how other people see you, and you are concerned that you will lose something. The sound of sadness is constantly reverberating in your mind, and in the depths of your inner mind, it is as if a helpless, powerless, but unneeded child is curled up. He is afraid of the darkness, and even more afraid of the unknown things lurking in the darkness. In the midst of this pain and suffering which seems so real, you almost want to give yourself a powerful hug, but you cannot find the object to hug. This is because it only exists in the endless false thoughts.

When the various false thoughts all stop, and your wisdom is no longer obscured, and you are able to go on and practice wondrous observing, it is then possible for the true mind to appear. It is like the clear bright sky emerging after the clouds have disappeared. It is like the ocean being like a mirror when the wind stops and the waves cease. But it is not enough for false thoughts to stop — there still has to be a light. What light? The light of wisdom. You cannot be as you are when you are about to fall asleep: at that time, although it is also empty and still, and you are not thinking of anything, that is a murky drowsy state. This is not the true mind, but rather a kind of inert emptiness. The true mind is empty and still, yet spiritually aglow, shining with light. It is like a crystal that can reflect light rays, and is very pure and clear, and yet is filled with the force of spiritual movements. This is why the true mind is also called bright emptiness.

To abide in peace in the bright emptiness, to abide in peace in the true mind, to let the light of the wisdom that reaches everything illuminate your life and transform your mind and spirit — this is the best form of cultivating practice.

Life Changes Because of Wisdom

With wisdom observing, you will live a serious, focused life, but without demanding results, and without demanding that a certain state remain forever. At this time, you can abide in peace in the inherent nature of phenomena, and go along with circumstances, and remain calm no matter how you are treated.

We who live in the mundane world of the red dusts inevitably come in contact with various kinds of evils, especially in this contemporary era of unlimited access to information. Therefore, in order that we not be subjected to the defilements of evil, we must build for ourselves a good environment. You must find a teacher who leads you toward the good, or form relationships with friends who are going toward the good, or always be reading good books which convey the spirit of great good, or always be doing the good things that are in your power to do, or use the forms of Buddhist practice, and thus let good information continuously influence your mind.

The human mind and spirit is like a field. If we do not plant crops, then weeds will grow there. If you do not use the true principles of generosity and bring benefits to living beings to influence your own mind and spirit, they will be filled with passive, negative information. If you want to live happily and calmly, you must choose appropriate content, choose some good methods, and plant truth and love in the field of your mind. By the same principle, if you are disgusted by certain phenomena in society, the first thing to do is let yourself change so that you are not the same way. Then use all you say and do to transmit the great good. When the voices of good in this society surpass the voices of evil, they will form a kind of good collective unconscious, and then this world will change. Thus it is said that changing the world starts with every one of you who is willing to change yourself.

In my novel *The Grey Wolf of Xixia*, there is a singer from the northwest of China, and he has killed countless dogs. Later, on a certain moonlit night, he is moved by the crying of a mother dog, and he suddenly understands that dogs too are living beings, and dogs too have mothers and children, and the mothers also feel unbearable pain when the children die. He had not known what a mother's love is, because his mother had died from giving birth to him. But he realized that when he was wounded or died, his mother would have been like that mother wolf, and she would have given this kind of grief-stricken cry for him. Thus, at that instant, that mind of his, which had been filled with hatred, suddenly melted. Grief filled his mind and spirit, and he generated a mind of genuine, sincere repentance. From then on, he constantly recited sutras bearing the spirit of great love and great good, and washed away the defilements in his own inner mind countless times, until he finally changed into a man whose mind was filled with love.

In reality, love is required in every person's nature, and it is something inherent in the human mind. The reason we sometimes neglect it is because we have become deluded by desires and false thoughts, and we cannot recognize the true mind. When we attune our minds using the appropriate methods, and let ourselves become more and more tranquil, we will then see the love and wisdom that our own inner minds are inherently equipped with, and experience compassion no different from all the buddhas and bodhisattvas. This is the wondrous functioning of the true mind, and it is also the genuine bliss of emptiness. It encompasses the whole realm of emptiness. It is what we often speak of as "unconditional great compassion, the great mercy of sharing the same essence with all beings." If you want to genuinely understand this point, you must have a correct mindfulness. And the prerequisite for having this correct mindfulness is becoming enlightened, understanding the true mind, and seeing the light of reality.

What is the true mind? What is the false mind? I always say that the false mind is the mind with false thoughts floating around, and the true mind is the mind that is empty and still clear through.

With the false mind, emotions move in waves, and miscellaneous thoughts are flying around all over. The true mind is the mind that is fundamentally pure and clean.

When the true mind has no waves and no ripples, and is fundamentally pure and clear, like empty space; it is like a clear mirror that reflects the myriad things, yet remains as it is without moving, and still has that awareness there. The empty inherent nature is its essence, and awareness is its function. The empty inherent nature is changeless, and the awareness appears according to conditions. This then is correct mindfulness. When your mind is clear and empty and still as empty space, when your mind is like a clear mirror reflecting the myriad things, you must maintain correct mindfulness, you must preserve the enlightened inherent nature. You can try to listen to a far-off birdsong. Of course, your purpose is not to hear that birdsong, but rather to generate a lucid awareness.

The causal conditions for illuminating mind are not the same for everyone. One day a girl understood true mind while she was doing the Kurukulla dance. (Kurukulla is the Enlightening Buddha Mother visualized in Vajrayana.) At that time she was very intoxicated, and reached the point where things and self were both forgotten. At that moment, she was Kurukulla and the Kurukulla was her. Her mind was filled with happiness, and her mind and spirit were as bright and clear and free as the sky. In her mind there were no miscellaneous thoughts, and no arbitrary distinctions, so she was free and happy, and exalted and tranquil. At this time she saw her own true mind.

The true mind is also "the ordinary mind" in the saying "the ordinary mind is the Path." It is a spiritual light with which we are all inherently equipped: clear and empty and still, shining bright, extending everywhere like space, reflecting everything like a clear mirror. When this light illuminates our lives, we then abide in peace in a kind of expansive calm adaptability, letting nature take its course as we live, and doing things following the true mind, without scheming or calculating, without so-called clinging or letting go. We do not put anything in our minds, and yet we can still act with complete focus and do anything well. This is what I often speak of as "using the mind that transcends the world to do tasks in the world." The "ordinary mind" is this mind that transcends the world.

If for the time being you cannot find a teacher who can enable you to become enlightened, you can still continuously observe the apparent forms of birth and extinction: the dewdrops evaporating; the flashes of lightning as they suddenly come and go; friends and loved ones who suddenly become ghosts worlds away; memories constantly changing into dogs fleeing into the desert; ancient cities that end up being swallowed by the sands; the beauty of the Maldives becoming a faded memory... With continuous observation, you will gradually understand the truth of the inherent emptiness of causal origination: whether you want it to or not, when old causal conditions scatter, and new causal conditions come together, the world will inevitably change. The changing illusory impermanence of the world will make you feel more and more indifferent to everything. Whether toward money, or fame and fortune, or gain and loss, and even including life itself, you will no longer care that much. But this not caring does not mean giving up without trying, but rather the wisdom in which there is no frantic seeking and no clinging or attachment.

With this wisdom observing, you will live a serious, focused life, but without demanding results, and without demanding that a certain state remain forever. At this time, you can abide in peace in the inherent nature of phenomena, and go along with circumstances, and remain calm no matter how you are treated.

What is the inherent nature of phenomena? The inherent nature of phenomena is the true face of the world. It does not change according to the birth and extinction of causal conditions. It is true thusness, the true mind, the real characteristic. It is the only eternal thing in the world. What is called using wisdom to change your life is recognizing the inherent nature of phenomena, preserving your awareness of the inherent nature of phenomena, and then gradually merging with the inherent nature of phenomena. When the inherent nature of phenomena is you, and you are the inherent nature of phenomena, the state of your life will spontaneously change.

Preserve Pure Awareness, Listen to the Voice of the Inner Mind

Preserve the pure awareness of your brain, and make sure your mind is always there at all times. At every moment you must clearly understand that there is no way of changing the past, and that everything in the future is built on the foundation of every moment here and now. You just have to do the tasks at hand with a peaceful mind, and listen to every sound that resonates from the inner mind, but you must not take these as directions you must obey.

Many times your mind decides the scene that appears before your eyes, and the appearance of every scene originates from your mind. When you are happy, you feel that the sunlight is bright and beautiful, and everything is sparkling. When you are not happy, you feel that everything is disgusting, and when a little bird is actually singing a song for you, you take a slingshot and shoot at it, saying the bird was bothering you. There is a poem that goes like this:

Hit out at the oriole,

Don't let it twitter on the branch.

When it warbles, it startles the concubine from her dreams,

And she cannot reach western Liaoning.

What the poem is speaking of is this kind of situation. In the mind of that lovelorn woman, when the beautiful bird was calling, it became an irritating sound that woke her up from her beautiful dream.

Therefore we say, whatever kind of mind you have, you will see that kind of world. Is your view of it the true characteristic of the world? It is and it isn't. For you, it is, because it exists in how you see it at a certain moment in time. For the world, it is not necessarily so, because the world is not the same in everyone's eyes, and everyone's way of looking at it is itself constantly changing. A certain friend once said that he thought the last sage in the world was (the Confucian statesman and scholar) Zeng Guofan (1811–1872), but I told him that Zeng Guofan had killed many people, and the common folk all called him Shaven-Headed Zeng. After this, my friend no longer regarded Zeng Guofan as a sage. So then, what is the true characteristic of the world? It is flowing water, it is cells that are born and die off in seconds, it is change, it is emptiness. Understanding that the fundamental substance of the world is emptiness is not to say that all our actions are meaningless, nor does it signify that we must abandon everything, and do nothing. Rather, it implies that we must and we can experience human life with the mental attitude that we are experiencing a dream.

Let's take an example. Since I know that worldly things are impermanent, and I can experience the bliss of that purity by myself, why do I still have to write this book? Why do I still have to say so many things? Why don't I hide in the mountains like a hermit, or simply go home and grow crops? It is because I know that many people are living very painful lives as they do not understand the true characteristic of the world, and I would rather take my momentary life and use it to follow the examples of the Buddha, Confucius and other sages of ancient times, and do something that benefits society, and say something that benefits society, and within this limited human lifetime, build something of true value. Of course, society may or may not be able to benefit from this, and all I can do is adapt to circumstances. This is what Buddhism calls "going along with the world."

Many people think that the Buddhist notion of going along with the world means submitting to adversity, but in fact it is not so. When Buddhists propose going along with the world, they are recommending that people, on the basis of accepting their own fates in life as a whole, make the decision for themselves to choose wisdom. They must not forget the reasons why, or blame things on everyone else, and they must not let the world that is changing a thousand times in the blink of an eye change their own clear understanding and happiness.

What is true wisdom? How can you judge whether you have chosen wisdom, or passive escapism, or impulsive false action? Buddhism recognizes that if you have clearly understood the true mind, and you can use the true mind to do things at every moment, and you have no delusions and no bonds at all, then you are a genuine person of wisdom, and you are choosing wisdom in every move you make.

So then, how can we put a stop to false thinking, and how can we know whether or not we are in the state of true mind?

In the sutras it has been said that at the same time we stop false thoughts, we can enter the state of true mind. The prerequisite for stopping false thoughts is that you must focus your attention on the things in front of you, and preserve pure wakefulness, and constantly observe the world of your own inner mind. This is also what we always speak of as "giving rise to alert awareness" and "maintaining the enlightened inherent nature." This is because it is only when you are totally aware of the state of your inner mind, that you know whether or not you are engaged in chaotic thoughts, and only then can you speak of stopping false thoughts.

If you discover yourself having false thoughts, how should you handle them? You should not use another thought, for instance, "I must not engage in chaotic thoughts," to try to repress them. Just do the things you must do, and treat those thoughts as passersby. You clearly see them coming, but you do not start chatting with them, much less curry favor with them: you just quietly watch them go. "You watch the swans go, hand strumming the five strings, content wherever you are, the wandering mind dark and mysterious." You let the thoughts come and go by themselves. This way, they will not create any disturbances for your mind, and you will not stir up even more waves because you want to suppress one wave. This also means that you will not disturb the tranquility of your own inner mind by making overly vehement distinctions between true and false.

I'll give you an example. You are writing a certain plan, and because you need to refer to similar cases, you go online and look for related information. But as you are searching for information, you see some news you feel is interesting, and so you put aside the job at hand, and browse through some web pages. While you are browsing through the web pages, you also begin to think of something you want to buy, and so you log onto a shopping website, and after spending some time there you realize, hey, my plan is still not finished yet! You look at your watch, and actually several hours have gone by, and you start blaming yourself for this...

Why is it like this? Because you were dragged off by the thought "I want to read the news," and you kept on following this thought and the many other thoughts that this thought spawned, and went further and further, and completely forgot what you had been doing, and of course you also forgot the importance of the task. If you could have let that thought come and go by itself at the start, without going along with it, and also without driving it off, then the whole chain of events that came next would not have happened. This is why we say that the best method for dealing with false thoughts is to not follow them off, and manage it so that "when thoughts come, you do not cling to them, and when thoughts go, you do not follow them."

If you have never observed the world of your inner mind, and you are not too clear about how specifically you must "observe" it, it is best to start by paying attention to your thoughts. Preserve the pure awareness of your brain, and make sure your mind is there at all times. At every moment you must clearly understand that there is no way of changing the past, and that everything in the future is built on the foundation of every moment here and now. You just have to do the tasks at hand with a peaceful mind, and listen to every sound that resonates from the inner mind, but you must not take these as directions you must obey. But this kind of listening cannot be too deliberate. If it is too deliberate, it will become another false thought. Paying attention and listening is done in order not to follow the false thoughts — not in order to take one false thought to repress another false thought, and not in order to create a new dualism.

But why is it that we must pay attention to false thoughts, and not directly recognize the true mind? It is because, for people who are first learning "observing," there may be some difficulty here too. The true mind is something that transcends concepts, so it is very hard for you to recognize it by learning concepts. Even if you are in the state of true mind for a few moments, you will still not dare to believe it, or else you will not be able to recognize it. Luckily the true mind and the false mind are two faces of a single essence, and when the false mind stops, what appears must be the true mind.

Where There Are No Thoughts, Preserve a Spiritually Alive Awareness

Between this thought and the next thought, there is a state where there are no thoughts, and if only you can catch it in time, and use your inherent nature or your awakened mind to observe it, you will very easily merge into the state of true mind.

The essential nature of the true mind and the false mind is one. They are not divided into two fundamental essences. It is just like the ocean when it is flat and still, and when the waves arise — although seen from the outside they are not at all the same, it is not true that there are two entities independent of each other. The essential nature of both of them is the sea water. When there is no wind, no waves arise, and only when you throw a stone into the water, do ripples form. The essential nature does not change, but because specific conditions differ, they produce many kinds of appearances.

When you cannot resist the delusive enticements of this world, and your mind follows your thoughts, your mind creates changes — this is the false mind. When the waves cease, this is the state of true mind. Everyone can experience this state of true mind at times, but we might not necessarily be able to recognize it. For example, between this thought and the next thought, there is a state where there are no thoughts, and if only you can catch it in time, and use your inherent nature or your awakened mind to observe it, you will very easily merge into the state of true mind.

Direct Explanations of the True Mind by the Korean Zen master Chinul (1158–1210) offers us ten excellent methods of "the true mind stopping the false."

First, vigilant observation. At the same time you are observing, you guard against false thoughts arising. As soon as you discover that you are engaged in random thoughts, you immediately cut them off, and do not keep thinking them. Say you are writing an article, but suddenly you begin to think of dinner, and you do not know what would be good to eat. At this moment you cannot linger over this question — rather, you must immediately return to the state of writing the article, and with focused attention, do a good job at the task at hand. You certainly must learn how to ward off those thoughts that are constantly enticing you, and above all, you cannot go off following them. This is because as soon as you relax your vigilance, these thoughts will use all kinds of reasons to come delude you, seduce you, and make you have doubts and waver in your own resolve.

Second, stopping — this is letting go. Let your discriminating mind come to a stop, and do not use it to evaluate the people and things in front of you. Do not calculate what is good and not good, what you must do and what you must not do, what is reliable and not reliable. After you observe, you let it go—that's it. For example, you see a beautiful woman, and after you appreciate her beauty, stop there. You do not evaluate whether her actions match her beautiful appearance, and you do not ponder what is most beautiful about her, and you must not keep thinking about her and become lovesick.

Third, letting the mind vanish and letting the objects remain. When false thoughts arise, you let them be obliterated. No matter what is happening externally, you just stop your own mind. If the false mind is extinguished, there will be no way for the external world to keep on deluding you or seducing you. For example, you see your own girlfriend eating a meal with another man, you are very unhappy, and you even feel hatred and anger. You are worried you will lose her, but this is just speculation on your part, and it only hurts you. Therefore, you might as well not do any speculating. Seeing is seeing, and if you do not do any imagining, worrying, or clinging, you can certainly manage not to fall into the fiery ocean of false thoughts.

Fourth, letting the objects vanish and letting the mind remain. All you have to do is clearly understand that all things are like mirages, and sooner or later become memories. These memories end up dissolving away too, and so you do not care about them.

Fifth, letting the mind vanish and letting the objects vanish. You not only understand that all things are empty and illusory and unreal, you also must understand that your own mind is the same way, going through myriad changes every moment. The things you are worrying about today are sometimes precisely the things you will be looking forward to tomorrow. The things you were looking forward to yesterday, may become the things you will be worrying about the day after tomorrow. This is because your emotions are changing all the time, and the world in your mind is changing all the time too. So why should you put external objects in your mind, and why should you spend so much mental energy thinking all kinds of thoughts about external things?

Sixth, letting the objects remain and letting the mind remain. You must not be deceived by the apparent forms before your eyes, and you should not go through various emotions like joy and loathing based on your experiences. If you can manage this, you will realize a genuine freedom. When I gave a lecture at the French Academy, I said that the external world lets us do what we want to do, and say what we want to say, but this is not true freedom. This is because it is passive; it requires cooperation from the external world, but this cooperation is not something we can control. Therefore, if we expect this kind of freedom, it is tantamount to acknowledging that we are slaves of the external world, and this is a great lack of freedom. It is only when our own world and the external world are independent of each other, and we are completely clear about everything that happens in the external world, but are not influenced by it, that we can finally realize true freedom and independence. This is letting the objects remain and letting the mind remain.

Seventh, internal and external as the whole essence. The myriad forms of the world are not apart from the true mind. A German philosopher named Martin Buber wrote a book called *I and Thou,* and in it he expounded on two possibilities for realizing something enduring: the first is to let a greater existence dissolve away the self, and the second is to let your own mind and spirit change into something sufficiently vast to be able to encompass the whole universe and the natural world. Just think, if your mental capacity were big enough to take in the whole external world, the external world and you would surely merge into one essence. Once you were fundamentally one essence, how could there still be any trace of dualism? If there is no dualism, then naturally there is no discrimination. If there is no discrimination, naturally there is no soil to nurture false thoughts. Of course, the prerequisite for realizing this inclusiveness is still to understand that the world is no more than a dream, an illusion, a bubble, and its fundamental substance is emptiness. But this is not the "emptiness without a single thing." Rather, it is like the true mind, an emptiness that has countless possibilities.

Eighth, internal and external as the whole function. When you can really abide in peace in the true mind, all external things, together with your own mind and thoughts, become the wondrous function generated by the true mind. You do not do any conscious analysis of them; you do not evaluate them by using thoughts, experiences, standards, or concepts; you do not use dualistic concepts to distinguish among them or draw conclusions about them. This means that when you are walking, you are walking, and when you are waking up, you are waking up, and when you are eating food, you are eating food. You do not add all sorts of goals and methods and evaluations to these very natural behaviors. For example, you do not calculate if your manner of walking is elegant or not, or if you grind your teeth when you sleep, or if people will laugh at you for eating too much. All you have to do is preserve your relaxed independence in the moment, and that will do.

Ninth, what is essence is function. Since the myriad phenomena before you are the essence of the true mind, they are also the function of the true mind. For example, when there is a big hole in the sidewalk, you go around it, and when you smell that the rice is sour, you know it has spoiled. But these are not false thoughts; rather, they are a direct perception that transcends concepts and consciousness. This kind of pure clear awareness is the difference between the true mind and being oblivious, being in a daze, being in a trance. You must preserve this pure lucid awareness at every moment, and at the same time abide in peace in a state of empty stillness. When you can experience the ease and independence of "emptiness," and you can also respond with agility to the things you may encounter, what need is there to create so much speculation and concern about things and events?

Tenth, penetrating through essence and function. You do not concern yourself with what is essence and what is function, what is true and what is false, what is external and what is internal, what is affliction and what is enlightenment. You take all concepts and dualistic distinctions and completely abandon them. You do not think of before and after, all you do is focus on the present moment, and stay pure and clear in the present moment. When you go along like this, you naturally will not create false thoughts.

These ten methods are all very good ways of entering into the Path. You must choose the one that is most appropriate for you, and cultivate practice according to the method over a long period. Then you will surely be able to see an enormous change in your mind and spirit, as well as in your life. Unfortunately, not many people recognize what has real value. Most people think what is truly valuable is to develop a facade and a pose that shocks the world, and they are always hidden in an occult remoteness, so the jewel is stained with dust, and the clear mirror is covered with dirt — this is really regrettable.

Understand That Life Is Like a Dream, and Treat Yourself and Other People Well

When you clearly understand that your own clingings and the things you cling to are all capriciously changing, and none of them can last forever, your mind will naturally relax, and relax again, and finally you will be as comfortable and pleased as if you are lying on the green grass under the warm sun. Then you will not feel that you are living such a fatiguing life, and you will be able to face this world and the things you go through, calmly taking things as they come. Then you will truly be solid and unbreakable.

When you are in the state of empty, still clarity, you will discover that all kinds of experiences pass. Once they pass, they are all just recollections. If you cling to a certain painful experience, your recollection will prolong the harm it did to you. If you do not concern yourself with it, then it is no more than a dream, an illusion, a bubble, without any substantive difference from the experiences that made you happy. These are just some fragments on your road of life, transient and fleeting, and together they form traces and evidence of your life.

Thus we say that people who cling to personal gains and losses will always generate afflictions and sufferings more easily than people who are unselfish. This is because they always have too many desires and cannot satisfy them all. They care about how other people see them, and they care about the world's attitude towards them. They care about whether or not they will get paid back for the efforts they expend. They always hold tight too many empty illusory forms, and are unwilling to let go of them. They always think that this is a way of being shrewd and lucid, and do not think it is worth reflecting on whether this may be another kind of fallacy. But they do not understand that the source of pain and suffering is precisely all this concern and shrewdness. Since they cannot see through this, of course they are not really people who are lucid, who really love themselves, or who understand how to love others. They may or may not manage to achieve much worldly success, but what is certain is that, adept in calculating as they are, they are sure to lead very fatiguing lives.

If you want to resolve or avoid afflictions, you must remember that when all entities in the world are appearing in your mind's nature, your true mind must be forever sensitive and clear, and must not become dimmed and muddled. That means when you are facing the world, you must constantly maintain tranquility and lucid awareness, and focus on and observe every thought of the inner mind. Do not let things with their many complex changes drag your mind away. Do not let yourself go and sink into certain emotions. Do not fall into oblivion, so there is no responsiveness at all. Only then will you no longer be controlled by false thoughts like concepts, experiences, desires, biased perceptions, and so on.

Of course, this is simple to describe in principle, but few people can truly manage to do this. People who can truly control their own minds, accept impermanence, clearly understand the world's illusory transformations, and not be controlled by false thoughts — they are the genuine people of wisdom. Only the genuine people of wisdom can treat themselves and other people well.

"Treat yourself well and treat other people well" and "Only when you learn how to love yourself will you be able to understand how to love other people" — do these mean the same thing? They do, and they don't. Treating people well is a kind of love, because only when you have love and compassion in your mind, will you be able to genuinely treat yourself and other people well. From this perspective, the two statements do mean the same thing. So why is it also true that in a sense they do not mean the same thing? Because "love" is a word that is very easily misinterpreted.

What is it to genuinely "love oneself"? To say what you want to say, to buy the things you want to buy, to do the things you want to do, to be faithful to your own opinions and viewpoints no matter how wrong they are — is this loving yourself? For some people, this may be what love is, but this is a self-centered love. This kind of so-called love is very selfish, and as for its basic substance, it is just strong desire. People who believe in this kind of love will always use the petty self as the criterion for assessment: What will I gain? What will I lose? What can't I get? Will this world satisfy me? Will I feel despair? Will I feel isolation and loss? The contradiction is that resources are limited: if someone gets something, then someone else cannot get it. If you always take satisfying yourself as the criterion, when conflicts of interest arise, will you be able to genuinely love someone else? When you encounter setbacks or problems, you will feel resentful and full of affliction: is this genuinely loving yourself? If you try to love in this manner, it will be impossible for you to genuinely love other people. For example, when someone praises you or smiles at you, you will certainly be able to respond to that person with a friendly attitude. But if another person refutes your point of view in a group meeting, and does not think the results of your work are right, and even slanders you, then how will you act? Will you still love him? Of course, the love I am speaking of now is in a broader sense, and not the emotional love between lovers.

Thus it is said that if we are unable to face "loss" with the mindset of accepting "gain," it will be hard to avoid being tied up in negative emotions like fear, a sense of loss, a sense of isolation, and so on, and fall into empty illusory pain and suffering. Some people cannot get out of the shadow of pain and suffering, and so they kill themselves, or they use violent means to protest against the world or get revenge. But no matter the reason, those who commit violence ultimately will taste the evil fruit which they have planted the seeds of with their own hands, and what is awaiting them is still endless pain and suffering. Is it something that the external world imposes on us? It is not. The various kinds of things that the external world gives rise to are the results produced by the coming together of many conditions, and they themselves are not fixed and unchanging. Because of this, no fixed attributes exist either, including our views and feelings toward people and things.

Everything in the world, and all that appears, first affects our minds, and then what appears from our minds are the myriad forms of being that manifest the nature of mind. This means that the eyes, ears, nose, tongue, body, and conceptual mind perceive forms, sounds, smells, flavors, touches, and conceptualized phenomena, and then give rise to the visual consciousness, the auditory consciousness, the olfactory consciousness, the tongue consciousness, the body consciousness, and the conceptual consciousness. These six kinds of information form all our perceptions and judgments of the world. In other words, our consciousness of the world is formed from what we see, what we hear, what we smell, what we taste, what we touch, and what we think. In this, the eyes, ears, nose, tongue, body, and conceptual mind are called "faculties," (in Buddhist Chinese, rendered by the word "roots") because they are like the roots of a plant, from which things can "grow forth." However, the things they put forth are not visible to the physical eye, but rather a kind of information. This is termed "consciousness," and it is not the same as the corresponding "root" on which it is based, and this is classified into six categories: the visual consciousness, the auditory consciousness, the olfactory consciousness, the tongue consciousness, the body consciousness, and the conceptual consciousness. The objects that the sense faculties perceive and think about are called "the sense objects." They can stimulate our minds and spirits, and make us produce desires, and defile our original purity, and so they are also called "the dusts." These include all the people and things of the external world and all apparent forms, and they are classified as forms, sounds, smells, flavors, touches, and conceptualized phenomena, distinguished by what is perceived by the eyes, ears, nose, tongue, body, and conceptual mind.

It is evident that all the ways we look at and perceive the world are in reality false states of mind. That false mind is the result produced by your six sense faculties and six sense consciousnesses coming together as one with the external world. For example, your eyes see a woman, and you feel she is very pretty, and this gives rise to the false mind, and you want to make her your girlfriend. This is the result of the functioning of the sense faculty of the eye, and the visual consciousness, and external sense objects. Differences in the mind determine the content of consciousness, and external sense objects themselves are changeable, so this result is constantly changing. For this reason, I always say that "when the mind changes, the world changes."

I will give a simple example. When a young man clings to conventional worldly sentiments, he may fall in love with a young woman at first sight, then abandon everything to pursue her.

One day he may go through an experience like Khyungpo Naljor, the great master who is the protagonist of my novel *The Holy Monk and the Spirit Woman*. Khyungpo Naljor gave up everything and went off to India in a quest for truth; later he brought the truth and the teachings that he had found back to his homeland, the snowy regions of Tibet. He played a role in the history of the transmission of Buddhist culture that cannot be overlooked.

The young man in the example now feels that the woman's beauty is far less important than his great aspiration and his direction in life, and so then he gives up his attachments to the woman, and continues his quest for his dreams.

If you clearly understand this point, the burdens on your mind will gradually lessen on their own, because you will discover that even these so-called burdens are empty and illusory. The reason they can torment you is that you see them as very real. When you clearly understand that your own clingings and the things you cling to are all capriciously changing, and none of them can last forever, your mind will naturally relax, and relax again, and finally you will be as comfortable and pleased as if you are lying on the green grass under the warm sun. Then you will not feel that you are living such a fatiguing life, and you will be able to face this world and the things you go through, calmly taking things as they come. Then you will truly be solid and unbreakable.

The Clarity and Strength to Master Your Life Comes from the True Mind

Genuine unassailable wisdom is the pure clarity and lucid awareness of the inner mind. Genuine "clear emptiness" is the clarity within the emptiness, the emptiness within the clarity, the enlightened inherent nature not apart from the empty inherent nature. It is preserving a kind of clear shining awareness while keeping to the true mind. Losing the emptiness and losing the clarity are both incorrect. Clarity that has lost emptiness will have false thoughts flying around in confusion. Emptiness that has lost clarity will fall into dead stillness like a stone.

Although I have constantly emphasized that the world is like a dream, like an illusion, like a bubble, and you should not cling to it, and you must relax your mind and taste that quiet tranquility, still, you also must understand that this state of quiet tranquility is nevertheless not something you blindly sink into. You must preserve the light of a spiritually alive enlightened nature at all times. I am calling this "the clarity within the emptiness." In it, "emptiness" is completely knowing impermanence, and "clarity" means enlightenment, awakening. This phrase works well to resolve doubts about the "empty inherent nature."

Many people think that the Buddhist culture is very passive, because they take the "empty inherent nature" emphasized in Buddhism to mean emptiness as in "empty with nothing there." But true "emptiness" is definitely not like this. At the same time that Buddhism emphasizes impermanence, it also emphasizes the wisdom of enlightened inherent nature. I call it "awareness of spiritual clarity." This means that Buddhism definitely does not think that people must not think of good and evil, and live like hibernating animals. Rather, people must calmly accept this truth of impermanence, and they cannot fall into the mistakes of no longer thinking, of being unwilling to take control of themselves, of no longer acting, of letting themselves be manipulated by fate. In all sorts of lectures, presentations and interviews, I have always brought up the cultural proposition that "your fate is made by your mind, and great good shapes your mind." The root cause of this lies in the fact that the core wisdom of Buddhism gives us an autonomous mind and spirit, and the clear awareness and strength to build our lives and fates.

Buddhism recognizes that if we completely understand impermanence, it will help let us not be bound by the suffering of the sense of loss that comes with "not being able to have" and "no longer having." But we still can take good care of and enjoy the things we have at the moment, because we recognize a kind of "wondrous being," which is not an eternal existence. When we completely understand impermanence, it helps us abide in peace in a state of pure clarity and independence, and face up to and be aware of everything in the world with a mental state that is relaxed, tranquil, and joyful. This "being aware" shows that we accept the objects that we are aware of, and accepting these objects is accepting the existence of wondrous being.

So then, why do we most often emphasize "emptiness?" It is because when we emphasize clarity too much, many people will take "wondrous existence" as "really existing." Then they will lose emptiness, and forget impermanence, and think that the objects we are aware of not only exist in the present moment, but will exist always. This mistaken view inevitably brings about endless affliction and clinging. That's because it will take you away from the state of clarity and emptiness, and you will only face the world with some kind of logic and thinking. Although I do not deny the function of thinking and logic, we must clearly understand that they are not genuine wisdom. Sometimes your logic and the truths you understand are engaged in a constant battle with your emotions and biased views, and in this way you get farther and farther away from tranquility and peace. This is because things like logic and thinking and principles are, in their fundamental substance, just false thoughts. When you use one kind of false thought to suppress another kind of false thought, even if you can achieve a temporary peace, and you do not get to the point that you go on and on splitting hairs, it will be like forcing an inflated ball underwater: as soon as you let go of it, it will spring back even higher. Thus, reasoning is a method that leads people to abstract truths, but these abstract truths in themselves are not genuine wisdom, and are not a basis that will enable you to be calm and at peace. Genuine unassailable wisdom is the pure clarity and lucid awareness of the inner mind. Genuine "clear emptiness" is the clarity within the emptiness, the emptiness within the clarity, the enlightened inherent nature not apart from the empty inherent nature. It is preserving a kind of clear shining awareness while keeping to the true mind.

Losing the emptiness and losing the clarity are both incorrect. Clarity that has lost emptiness will have false thoughts flying around in confusion. Emptiness that has lost clarity will fall into dead stillness like a stone. Some people crave the feeling of emptiness: they relax their vigilance, and lose track of enlightened inherent nature. Then they will be like people wandering in a dream, with no way to be keenly aware of all that is in the world, and no way to make any spiritually sensitive responses to anything in the world, and no way to use wisdom to ward off the many challenges and assaults in life. As soon as provocations come from external objects — for example, a very appealing woman appears in your life, a woman you cannot get, or in your work you encounter some threat that has never been there before — your emptiness conspicuously collapses. Before you think of any abstract truths, the pain is already like water gushing through a broken dam, assaulting your mind and spirit. Unless you can wake up in time, and return again to the state of the true mind, you are still just like anyone who has never been enlightened, flowing along with the empty illusory feelings brought on by the stimulus of external objects, entangled in painful false forms like feelings of loss and hopelessness, unable to pull yourself out. Under the sway of desires, you may even do things that conflict with your principles of virtue. What Buddhism calls samsara, the cycling through birth and death, is born from this. Thus it is said that emptiness alone, or clarity alone, will let your mind develop problems — you must pay attention to this point.

But though I constantly emphasize the implications of many terms, in fact I do not hope that anyone will get tangled up in vocabulary. I do hope that you can use thinking and reflecting to make contact with your own mind and spirit, and recognize your own true mind. Vocabulary is just a signpost on the road: you must follow the directions on the sign to go toward enlightenment, not just remember what the sign looks like. In the *Diamond Sutra* it emphasizes over and over again that we must not become attached to forms, that forms are just a means of transmitting certain information to you, that they are tools and routes, but not the goal itself.

So then, what are these "forms?" "Forms" are the many texts in the sutras, the many stories in the Zen koans, the many things I say when I give lectures, the many tumultuous events in the world, and so on and so forth. All these are forms, and they are also manifestations, and external appearances. The concrete content of all these manifestations is not what is most important. What is most important is whether or not they can touch you, whether or not they can make you think, whether or not they can ignite the spiritual light of your inner mind. Therefore, whenever you are reading some books of wisdom, do not take "translating them" as your goal. Use your mind to go experience their inner truth, and taste and enter into that great ocean of wisdom that lies hidden behind the text. Only if you do this, will you avoid feeling confused by terms which appear repeatedly but with different concrete meanings, or by confused logic which at first sight appears contradictory. Only if you do this will you not be disoriented by the intricate complexities of the apparent forms of the world as they are born and die away again and again.

Build Something Relatively Eternal amid Empty Illusion

When you have understood the gap between the evanescence of life and the lasting values you want to build, and you actively design your own life and treasure every minute and every second of life, you will not pass through life in vain, you will not take the false as true, and you will not cling to the illusory as real. Only when you go on like this, will you be able to live out the true dignity and value of life, and bring to the world things of true beauty and benefit.

When you consider the false to be real, and you do not know that all things, including your physical body, are empty and illusory and impermanent, you will give rise to many desires and clingings. Then you will waste your life and money on utterly worthless things, and for the sake of more enjoyment, you may even hurt others to benefit yourself. This is why so many rare animals become delicacies for humans. This is why so many monkeys have the top of their skulls opened up and sprinkled with oil. This is why so many animals are skinned alive... When you have understood the principle that phenomena arising through interdependent causation are empty by nature, and you use this to direct your behavior, you will not cling to physical pleasures, and you will not commit endless murderous deeds in order to preserve the physical body which will ultimately disintegrate.

When you discover that the world's myriad things all decay, and are not eternal and unchanging, your inner mind may produce a feeling of intense fear. You might feel that living is meaningless, and everything is meaningless, because in the end everything disappears. This fear is like the shadow that a disaster film leaves with people: it makes us confront death directly, reflect on life, and reflect on the human lifespan. However, though we all know that everyone will die, why do so many people fear the approaching of the end of the world? This is generally because people have never really been conscious of how brief life is.

For example, we know that smoking is damaging to our health, and we know that reversing night and day is damaging to our health, and we know that constantly eating junk food is damaging to our health, and we also know of many other habits which do no good to our health, but we never seem to eliminate bad habits like these. Why is this? Because we always feel that death is some remote topic. For us, death seems like a bad dog standing on the other side of a river, and we do not fear it, just because we know it cannot cross over to us. But in fact, death is not like that bad dog on the other side of the river, because it can approach at any time.

A young friend once described to me the sudden death of a friend of his. Three years prior, he got a call from his friend, asking if he was going to go play soccer, and saying that he himself was already on the soccer field. Who could have known that a half hour later he would receive news of his friend's death? He said that at the time he was dumbstruck, because he never would have thought that his close friend would end up dying such an inexplicable death—he was still so young, how could he have died? How would his family cope with it? Had he ever been genuinely happy? Had he lived out the dream that was valuable to him? ...

When you become conscious that impermanence follows us like a shadow follows a form, and death can approach at any time, you may not instantly become enlightened, and you may have no way of abiding in peace in the inherent nature of phenomena. Your inner mind may be filled with an enormous fear. You fear the dissolution of causal conditions, you fear that everything in the world will lose its meaning for existing, and you are perplexed by this. Since in the end flowers will wither and fall, why should they still be in full bloom? Since people will ultimately die, why should they still live wonderful lives?

Whether it is the realm of desire, the realm of form, or the formless realm, any world will form, abide, decay, and become empty. Any world will decay and be extinguished. Any world is evanescent as a bubble. Any world is like a flower reflected in a mirror, or the moon reflected in the water. When you suddenly realize this, at the beginning you feel anxiety: you become aware that nothing in this world can be relied upon. Money, profits, fame, social status, houses, lovers, relatives, friends… all these things will disappear like dewdrops in the sunlight. The only thing that is constantly with you is that mind, which is still not yet enlightened, a spirit that is weak and afraid. At this time a powerful fear arises in your mind, an excess of fear, and you begin to directly face your own mind and spirit, because you want to find a way of living that will leave you with the least regrets. This is very similar to the mental state of a person who knows he has got a terminal illness. He discovers that so many things do not belong to him, and his chasing fame and profit was actually meaningless. He wants to know how he should go on living.

When you start to reflect on this, you can no longer go on living in ignorance, because this kind of reflection will change your whole attitude toward life, and influence all your choices. Many people who have changed their lives because of this call this period of questioning and awakening a "rebirth," being reborn by bathing in fire.

After this, you use this awareness to observe dangerous objects. What are dangerous objects? All things in the world that are unreal illusory transformations are dangerous objects.

The forms your eyes see are dangerous objects. The sounds your ears hear are dangerous objects. The flavors your tongue tastes are dangerous objects. It is the same principle. Sensations of touch are even more this way. When you talk of love and embrace and kiss, you feel a beauty and wonder beyond compare, but the instant you part, all these feelings of touch are totally lost. Even your own name is impermanent. Even if the whole world knows your name, after this generation of people dies off, your name will be buried along with you in your grave. And profit is even more impermanent.

It was precisely because of a realization of death, that I began to search for the meaning of life when I was ten years old. Even now I still put a human skull next to my pillow: it is the wake-up pillow in my life. It is also because of a lucid awareness of death that I always value every minute and every second of life, and constantly live in a kind of clarity and wakefulness. Although I go along adapting to conditions, I never go off chasing after the waves. I know that when people are alive, it is not to go toward death, and it is not for the sake of any enjoyments: rather, it is for the purpose of achieving something of value in the process of living. What is this thing of value? It is that this world should be better off with you than without you—this is your value. That's why I say that my writing has never been to please the public and win acclaim. I have never altered the style or the content of my writing for the sake of sales or fame. All I want is to use my time alive to write some good meaningful books, to enable the people reading the books to understand some truth. This is the way I make my own value real, and build something enduring in the midst of empty illusion. Of course, this being "enduring" is relative, it is not something eternal. One day when the earth is destroyed, there will be books no more, and even the human race may be no more. At that time, it will be an even greater dangerous object.

When you have understood the gap between the evanescence of life and the lasting values you want to build, and you actively design your own life and treasure every minute and every second of life, you will not pass through life in vain, you will not take the false as true, and you will not cling to the illusory as real. Only when you go on like this, will you be able to live out the true dignity and value of life, and bring to the world things of true beauty and benefit.

Plant the Seeds of Great Love in the Field of the Mind

Real Solitude Is a Realm of Experience

When you have become a lotus flower, and you look down at the pond, you discover that there are many lotus seeds in the pond which could have grown and born lotus flowers. But because of certain reasons, they fall into the mud, and cannot sprout. At this time, that lotus flower might be isolated. It hopes that all the lotus seeds can get beyond the mud. When it cannot realize this hope, it produces a feeling of solitude.

What is the true spiritual nature? The spiritual nature is freedom. Freedom goes beyond any "isms." It transcends any human concepts, limitations, and standards. It is transcendence. But then, what is transcendence? Transcendence is also freedom. What then is freedom? Freedom is transcending all human concepts. It is something attained after going beyond constraints like business suits, and bonds like neckties. This kind of thing is also called the true spiritual nature. In contemporary literature, it is already very difficult to see anything of transcendence. Why? Because in this era, various things exclude this topic for writers.

In 2004, I went to Romania to attend a session on international literature, and the theme of the session was "being solitary in the global village." More than one hundred and fifty authors from two dozen countries showed up, and everyone was talking about being solitary. But the solitude of which they spoke was the pressure put on writers by the contemporary media. They said that writers could no longer get a big response as in the past, and could no longer be as "exalted" as in the past. In short, they no longer had their past glory. This kind of "solitude" filled the whole of the literary world.

Later, when I was interviewed by an international broadcaster, I said that that the authors had said little about solitude, and what they had spoken of was not solitude, but rather a feeling of decline. I told the interviewer that I did feel the solitude. But what is my solitude? It is that I want to establish something eternal and imperishable, but there is nothing eternal in this world. We cannot find the eternal, we do not keep on existing forever, and we cannot possibly establish anything which time cannot destroy. But I persist in wanting to establish this kind of thing. An enormous gap forms here, and this is my solitude. I cannot resolve this issue, and the same goes for many writers and great philosophers. Thus, they are in pain. They feel that this world is disappearing swiftly toward someplace we do not know, and we cannot hold it back, nor can we keep any bit of the eternity we want to keep. It is precisely this kind of unresolvable issue that creates my solitude.

Because of this, for a long time I couldn't write, because I could not find meaning in writing. Although I felt this world might let my writings last forever, I knew that no one knows how long this world can last. This is because the human race has created nuclear weapons that can destroy the world countless times over, because there are so many people on earth who still madly compete to seize the world's resources, and destroy our home. One day a friend told me that the water level in Venice is rising, and that beautiful city may soon be under water. This world is rapidly fading away towards we don't know where, and yet I still want to establish something eternal. This kind of solitude is an issue the human race cannot resolve.

My solitude is not that I cannot earn a lot of money, or get a lot of profit and fame, and not that television and the Internet are putting pressure on print media. These kinds of things cannot create solitude. Solitude is something that comes from the inner mind. It has no connection with the world. When an author is too concerned about how the world sees him, he has already fallen. When he wants to get a beautiful girlfriend, but cannot, he may suffer. When he wants to have a great deal of money, and he wants to be as rich as Bill Gates, and he cannot have what he wants, he may fall. Feelings of loss are not solitude.

Solitude is a realm of experience, a very lofty realm. Jesus wanted to love humanity, he wanted to practice universal love, but this world was not willing to let him be that way, and wanted to crucify him. He would say: "Forgive them Lord, they know not what they do"—this is solitude. When Shakyamuni Buddha was enlightened beneath the bodhi tree, and he saw that so many people are deluded by empty illusory false forms that are in the midst of disappearing, and their minds are full of greed, hatred, and ignorance, and he saw that he would be unable to immediately enable these people to dispel this pain and suffering, he was in solitude. When Confucius in China put forth to the whole world his teaching of "human fellow feeling and love," but had no choice in the world of his time and kept fleeing from one place to the next like a lost dog, he was in solitude. Thus, true solitude is a realm of experience. People who cannot reach this realm can only be called those who have suffered a loss; they cannot be called in solitude.

When you have become a lotus flower, and you look down at the pond, you discover that there are many lotus seeds in the pond which could have grown and born lotus flowers. But because of certain reasons, they fall into the mud, and cannot sprout. At this time, that lotus flower might be isolated. It hopes that all the lotus seeds can get beyond the mud. When it cannot realize this hope, it produces a feeling of solitude. Solitude is this kind of thing. True solitude can only be produced after you have transcended the environment in which you exist.

I was looking for transcendence all along. Later I discovered that what spiritual yoga considers to be transcendence and freedom is not the same as the transcendence and freedom spoken of in Western philosophy. Why are they not the same?

The German philosopher Martin Buber wrote a book called *I and Thou*. He recognized two possible ways for humans to realize something imperishable. The first way is to dissolve the ego. When the whole vast universe and nature dissolves your own greed, ignorance and hatred, freedom can be produced. The other way is that freedom can be realized when our own minds and spirits encompass the whole universe and natural world, and our own minds become as vast and rich as the universe, and as broad and all-embracing as nature.

The freedom which Mahamudra Yoga seeks is the latter kind. It confronts our own minds and spirits, and wins the world by conquering our own desires. So is it not some kind of so-called freedom we realize by plundering and attacking, or taking something that we recognize as some kind of truth and forcing it on this world? No, it is not.

Mahamudra has always taken molding the spirit as the main task. This word "spirit" means the "spiritual nature." What literature truly pursues is precisely this.

The relationship of the spiritual nature and the spirit with material things is not that important. After the basic conditions for human survival are fulfilled, good fortune, freedom, and liberation are all decided by our own minds and spirits.

From our point of view, the life of people in the West is already very good. They have good food in their stomachs, nice clothes on their bodies, and also such a beautiful environment. How strange then, that there are so many people who feel pain, so many who suffer from depression and commit suicide, and even murder other people? For us it is very hard to understand where this pain and suffering is coming from.

My hometown is like the ocean of songs, and there are many songs there. Every song is a wave in the ocean. No one knows ultimately how many kinds of songs there are. We eat rice porridge, dumplings, corn and things like that, and we feel very happy. Why? Because nature has given us so many things, and enables us to survive, so naturally we are very happy. At these times, other than enjoying the happiness and the bright sunshine, we do not go to steal things from other people. When we can sustain life with a cup of water, we do not try to seize someone else's ocean. When we have an apple to eat, we take bananas and other fruit and let other people eat them, or keep them for their children and grandchildren to eat. We feel that it is not necessary to grab everything and put it in our own house. Thus, the freedom of practitioners of the Great Mudra is realized by dissolving away the greed, ignorance and hatred in their own inner minds. They can be unconcerned with how this world is, and still live very happily. The authenticity and spiritual nature of Chinese literature also lies here.

Use the Mind That Transcends the World To Do Things in the World

When everyone is seeking money, fame, profit and material things, but you can refuse them with a smile, and not let your own mind and spirit be subject to the control and bondage of all these enticements, this is transcendence. After you realize transcendence, you will discover that nothing is this world can compare to a truly independent, free mind.

What is called transcending the world does not mean not doing anything, but rather doing things after realizing transcendence. This means that your behavior must go beyond the limits of your petty "mind." You cannot take the concept of doing things and only use it with people who have connections with you; you must not have any conditions, then you must "use the mind that transcends the world to do things in the world." Transcending the world does not imply that you must not do things in the world, but rather requires that you not fall into the desires and afflictions of this world, but still do things.

Let's put it in another way. Bill Gates is so wealthy, but he has also gone beyond wealth. In his attitude toward wealth he has realized a kind of transcendence which the common person cannot understand, and money can no longer bind his mind, spirit and actions. He then expresses his realm of experience by entering into worldly affairs. Thus, transcending the world does not mean escaping from this world, and entering into the world does not mean falling into this world. Entering the world is drawing nutrition from this giant pond; transcending the world is growing a lotus flower in this pond. Transcending the world does not mean picking this lotus flower and blandishing it as a sign to deceptively win the acclaim of worldly people. When this flower does not have the pond, it will quickly wither, unless it is a false flower, something to trick worldly people and falsely win fame. The true flower of transcendence needs the nutrition that comes from the muddy and worldly pond. Everyone must throw his or her own life into the pond, to grow the true flower of his or her own mind and spirit. But we must not turn into tadpoles or eels or worms: we must go beyond and turn into lotus flowers.

When everyone is seeking money, fame, profit and material things, but you can refuse them with a smile, and not let your own mind and spirit be subject to the control and bondage of all these enticements, this is transcendence. After you realize transcendence, you will discover that nothing is this world can compare to a truly independent, free mind. The things we must pursue is precisely this mind, not those things which are so easily destroyed by time, like apartment buildings, cars and money.

Do children in West China need everyone's help? They do need it, but in their own minds they don't. What does that mean? Many people say that when Xuemo was young, he endured hardships, but fundamentally I had no hardships. Children in West China live happier lives than children in Shanghai. How much the children in Shanghai suffer—you see them going to classes on weekends, bearing the burdens their parents have loaded upon them. A father who has no possibility of an official post says to his child, "Son, in the future you must be a high official." The father himself cannot become a Warren Buffet, so he says to his child, "Son, in the future you must be a financier." How much weight is loaded onto the little backs of these children? So even if they have attained a Ph.D. degree, they may jump off a high-rise building, because they cannot bear the weight any more.

My son's name is Chen Yixin, and he did not go to college. When he was in elementary school, he said, "I do not want to do homework, I want to read books by myself." He said homework would waste too much of his time. I agreed, and I called up his teacher, and told him not to assign my son homework. When he was going into middle school, he said that there was so much schoolwork that he did not have any time to be himself, and he needed to read books. I said okay, then I called the school and told them not to make my son do schoolwork. Later on, when it was time for him to go to college, he said that he wanted to be a writer, and did not want to go to college. I said okay, then you don't have to go to college, and it will be fine if you become a writer.

When he was entering middle school, I discovered a love letter he had written to a girl: "My dear, in the future I will take you to Mount Fuji in Japan to look at the cherry blossoms." I said, "Son, it sounds great. But if some chance you cannot even fill your own stomach, that could be a problem." He said, "Certainly I will be able to fill my stomach." He was not wrong in what he said. So far I have brought my son along to many places, and all my friends tell me, "Your son is very healthy, and outstanding. He could give lessons to many college students." A while back, he set up a literary institute in West China, and many young people studied writing with him. If he had continued with this, he could have made a lot of money. But later he did not want to keep doing this: he said that he wanted his life to develop a greater value, that he wanted to write. I agreed, and told him: "If you do not want to be an official, then you should not be an official — do something you like. As long as you have a noble character, as long as you can bring true goodness and beauty to this world, then whatever you do, your father will support you." In other words, as long as a person intends to go higher, no matter what sky he flies toward, it is always worthy of our praise.

On this point, children in Shanghai are not as fortunate as children in West China. So if someone asks, do the children in

West China need our concern? Of course they don't. They do not know that the outside world is concerned with them, because they are very happy. When they see the stars, when they experience the chatter of the birds and the fragrance of the flowers, they are very happy. When I am flying along on a swift steed, and many people give me envious looks, I am so fortunate. When people say to me, "You went through such suffering in your childhood," and I always reply, "I did not suffer, I did not feel I was suffering. All this suffering is something you told me about." Most of the hardships of the people in West China are things they are told about by people from East China. In fact, the former group is very happy. Therefore, when you are concerned about the people of West China, you tend to have the best intentions, you want to change them, and everyone praises you. But this sort of help should be a dialogue between the two regions. Don't disturb them, don't discriminate against them. You should try to understand the way they live. West China draws nourishment from the culture of East China, and East China draws greater and more glorious nourishment from the culture of West China. When these two cultures join forces, this world will be more beautiful, and I feel it will be this way.

To Do Well in the Present Moment Is the Best Ultimate Concern

We do not just rebuild the homes of people who have survived disasters: even more necessary is to rebuild the home of the mind and spirit, and treat everyone around us well. When they need help, we extend a helping hand. When they are beset with afflictions, we give them a smile, and all the loving concern we are capable of. We give them the help that can refresh them and enable ourselves to reach a higher level.

Apart from the world-transcending truth, there is nothing eternal in the world, and the world cannot have anything eternal. Therefore, what we speak of as the ultimate concern means that the past has already dissolved away, and the future will end up dissolving away, and what we can hold onto is just the present moment. In this present moment that you can take hold of, you must do things that are useful to the people around you, that are useful for the world, and that can bring benefits to the human race. You must enable the world to extend the time that humanity will exist—this is the true ultimate concern. Besides this, are you able to leave something imperishable for this world? Being able to accomplish this is also the ultimate concern.

This is because everything before our eyes is all changing, and dissolving away. Since we know that nothing can last forever, can we establish anything that is relatively imperishable, relatively everlasting, in the midst of this irresistible flood? Pondering this point enables some people at last to find the meaning of being alive. Some people ask me what kind of person I am, and I tell them I am a great fool. They ask me why I say this. I say I clearly understand it cannot be done, and yet I do it. This is because I want to realize a kind of existence amid the emptiness, and establish something eternal amid the impermanence, and realize something imperishable amid the empty illusions—I want to nurture some great teachers in the heap of confusion and chaos. I clearly know this cannot be done, but I insist on doing this. The nobility of the human race is precisely this. It is hard for the human race to change its own life, because the universe too has a lifespan. When we can change our own minds and spirits and attitudes, this is the very best ultimate concern.

At the time of the devastating earthquake in Wenchuan, a friend said that so many people in our nation showed great concern. I told him that our compassion and sympathy does not need a disaster to be awakened, and does not have to be aroused at the cost of so many lives. In the present moment, we can all be concerned with our family members, our friends, everyone around us, the environment, and we can try to live in harmony with nature. If it takes the occurrence of a disaster to stimulate one's mind of sympathy, then we would rather not need this kind of sympathetic mind. But this is a paradox. If there were no sympathy or compassion or love in the world, then all kinds of disasters would occur. For example, the human race is ceaselessly harming the environment, building all kinds of weapons to slaughter their fellow humans, exploiting natural resources without restraint, and so on — all these things could bring on countless disasters. The present day earth is already riddled with wounds. We must clearly understand that our sympathetic mind should not be evoked only by earthquakes, or by the faces of countless people who are injured and suffering, or by disaster scenes of corpses and ruins.

In fact, in the mind of every person, there is a seed of good. Our ancestral teachers call this the good mind. Every person has the good mind. When a disaster occurs, everyone discovers his own good mind. In fact, humans all belong to this earth, and we all have the power of life. So then, can we or can we not stop creating the "causes" that bring on disasters? Can we or can we not extinguish the flames of desire in our minds, distance ourselves from greed and hatred, and stop polluting the world and humanity? Can we stop relentlessly exploiting natural resources, stop creating spiritual and material trash, and let our minds become more compassionate?

This is why we must let every medium that has the power to influence people, every person with the power to speak to the masses(we call them experts and scholars), and every organization that disseminates culture gradually spread the ideals of the good mind and compassion. Let the mind of sympathy evoked by disasters become a living habit for all of us, as inseparable from our lives as breathing.

We do not just rebuild the homes of people who have survived disasters: even more necessary is to rebuild the home of the mind and spirit, and treat everyone around us well. When they need help, we extend a helping hand. When they are beset with afflictions, we give them a smile, and all the loving concern we are capable of, and give them the help that can refresh them and enable ourselves to reach a higher level.

But this kind of communication, this kind of help, must also adapt to circumstances, and must be a dialogue between the two areas based on the common principles of living together in peace. During one interview someone asked me: "If the wisdom of Buddhism is so great for the human race, why haven't the Buddhists put their truth into practice by establishing political power?" I told him that although in history, there were many rulers who believed in Buddhism, and used worldly power to spread Buddhism, e.g. King Ashoka in India, Buddhism is dedicated to adapting to causal conditions, and it respects all forms of thought. If Buddhists put their own ideas into practice through coercive power, then it would be no different than other people's despotism. Cultural despotism, despotism over thought, despotism over the spirit—any form of despotism is the great enemy of humankind. Thus Buddhism has always respected the culture of other countries, and has never resorted to bloody methods to spread its own teachings. Because people differ in their basic capacities, they require different cultural nourishments. Different people have different ways of life and different ways of thinking. However you want to live, Buddhism respects you. The wisdom of Buddhism is like the sun: it does not discriminate between the poisonous herbs and the fragrant flowers. No matter what kind of living thing it is, the sun will give them all the same warmth and light.

As for how much you can absorb, that must be determined by your root capacity and your enlightened nature. Buddhism is a kind of observation of wisdom, rathen than a crude assault, and it pays very close attention to causal conditions. When it has the support of the rulers, that is no doubt good, but when it does not have their support, that is no big problem. If someone yearns for power in order to spread a religion, and extends their violence in the process, that is another kind of greed—and evil. Buddhism does not think that its own religion can replace other religions: the ills of the human mind and spirit are not the same, and so, however many kinds of sickness there are, there need to be that many medicines.

Buddhist wisdom recognizes that in the long river of infinite time, all living things may have been our mothers during a certain lifetime in the cycle of birth and death. The Buddhist scope of mind is something even broader and greater.

Take this book as an example. If you read this book, you may have the realization that life is a bit better than yesterday, and someday you will tell someone else about your realization, or write to someone and have him read it, and this person may detach from clinging as a result, and become a bit more intelligent and compassionate. This is my goal in writing this book. But I certainly will not run into the street saying these things to whomever I happen to see — if I were to do this, other people would definitely think I was crazy. I pay very close attention to causal conditions.

There are many kinds of greedy desires in the world, and to cling to a certain teaching without paying attention to causal conditions is also a kind of greed and affliction.

Fundamentally, There Is No Conflict Between Believing It and Putting It into Practice

True dignity in life is a matter of a person having true yearning. Yearning for what? Yearning for something greater than oneself, some existence loftier than oneself. Only when a person preserves his or her reverence for a certain spirit, can the person yearn for it. The highest reverence is not a slavish state of mind, but rather a form of yearning, an embodiment of the realm of wisdom.

Many friends view faith as something that exists independent of life, but in fact this is wrong. I have said that when the lotus has been removed from the pond, unless it is an artificial flower, it will surely wither. All faith, all states of mind that transcend the world, only have meaning when they take action within the world.

There was a young person who said to me that he wanted to live better, so he had to accept many conventional worldly things, and he could not do more elevated things like being a volunteer, or else it might be difficult even to survive. I said to him: "When you decide something is conventional or not, in fact this is your own discriminating mind playing tricks. You should not concern yourself with whether something is conventional or not—you just have to attend to whether your intent is good or not. I'll give you an example. When a beggar reaches out his hand to you, can you or can you not treat him with the attitude you would use when dealing with your boss or your parents? Do not look upon daily life as something worldly and conventional, and working as a volunteer as something lofty and noble. You must always treat people with the ordinary mind. In your mind you must maintain a kind of good thought, then you will achieve this. Even if you work as a lawyer, and someone hires you for a lawsuit, this is fundamentally a worldly transaction, but when you use a good mind to deal with him, help him, and get him to better understand how to treat other people well, this kind of worldly transaction still goes far beyond the conventional world. I too am very worldly. In my hometown, when some people are talking about me, they say: "This guy Xuemo really earns a whole lot of royalties!" I definitely do not always give people a feeling of holiness—it's just that I have managed to be very happy with or without money. I definitely do not use my life, my freedom, and my dignity to earn money. When you can get to this point, naturally you will no longer be controlled by this world.

Many people feel that in this period when market conditions are very bad, and competition is very fierce, if you want to have money, then you must pay the price in morality. If your moral standards are high, you may suffer poverty, and in the end you still may be wiped out by people whose minds are permeated by greed and desire. But I am telling you, human desires are endless, and most of today's so-called development, is in reality an attempt to satisfy these endless human desires. This is why, whether it is the development of an individual person, or the economic development of a society, what it brings to humankind is affliction. For example, the more contemporary science develops, the quicker humanity might be annihilated, because it wastes so many energy resources, and when so many energy resources are wasted, humans will build nuclear power plants, covet the rich natural resources of other nations, and go on and develop nuclear weapons. Then this world has more conflicts and more chaos caused by war, and when nuclear energy gets out of control, it will bring an enormous disaster to the whole human race.

In the eyes of a greedy person, there are always things he does not yet have, and he always wants to have them. This mental state of "seeking" makes it impossible for him to ever live so that he can be relaxed and happy. On the other hand, those who know how to be satisfied with what they have are always happy. Many people in West China, even though they live in the mountains and have little to eat and dress very plainly, feel a sense of good fortune that is no less strong than people who live in the great cities. This is because, after satisfying the basic conditions for survival, a person's good fortune has nothing to do with material things — it is just related to the state of the person's mind and spirit. Whether or not your state of mind is harmonious, whether or not your mind and spirit are at peace — this and nothing else determines the quality of your life.

Happiness is this way, and so is dignity. Some people feel that if they are rebuked by someone else, then they have lost their dignity. In fact, being susceptible to being hurt by other people is not a matter of dignity, but of face, of vanity. Genuine self-respect is a steadfast strength of the inner mind, a calmness that comes after you realize independence of the mind and sprit. This kind of thing cannot be taken away by someone else rebuking you or attacking you. So do not think that if you have no money, you cannot be happy, that if you have no money, then you have no dignity. As long as you have a mind that goes toward the good, and you forget about how much you have gained and lost, you will naturally live happily and with dignity. Only then will that which you realize be a kind of genuine dignity. The bodies of many large trees shake in a strong gale, but their roots still bite firmly into the ground, and after the wind stops, they will be the same as before — calm, steady, as if nothing happened. People must be like this too. Aside from true dignity and true value in life, all the other things like vain glory, praise, blame and so on are no more than a few memories, things that disappear in the blink of an eye, whether they are good or bad, whether you want to hold onto them or not, so they have no true meaning at all.

True dignity in life is a matter of a person having true yearning. Yearning for what? Yearning for something greater than oneself, some existence loftier than oneself. Only when a person preserves his or her reverence for a certain spirit, can the person yearn for it. The highest reverence is not a slavish state of mind, but rather a form of yearning, the embodiment of the realm of wisdom. Over a long time, you will develop something we call "confidence in your innate enlightenment," and you will have a firm belief that you are a buddha, that there is no duality between the self and the fundamental buddha. With firm belief you only have to firmly uphold the cultivation of practice, and then you will have a character as great as a buddha. When you truly have a character as great as a buddha, you will be as great as Shakyamuni Buddha. As long as you are not fully equipped with that kind of spirit, you must maintain your reverence and yearning for it. You cannot take the Buddha as a friend, because you cannot use all your life and spirit to yearn for the realm of a friend. You cannot abandon everything in life to focus on cultivating practice just to have a friend's spirit. When you take the Buddha as a friend, you are just appreciating him, and praising him, but you are not wanting to become him. If you are like this, then you cannot possibly change the condition of your life, and benefit from that.

Many people see Buddhism emphasizing over and over again that desire is the root source of suffering, and so they think Buddhist wisdom only has this one point. But this is incorrect.

This is just a drop of water, while Buddhist wisdom is a vast ocean. Buddhist learning is more than just a kind of learning, it is also a kind of spirit. Some people, like Lei Feng (1940– 1962), Kong Fansen (1944–1994) and others, did not believe in Buddhism, but they had the kind of spirit which Buddhism advocates — the bodhisattva spirit of benefitting living beings. Buddhism considers such people bodhisattvas too. This is because Buddhism is something that transcends names and forms. In the *Diamond Sutra* Buddha says: "If someone sees me in terms of form, or seeks me by sound, this person is traveling a misguided path, and will not be able to see the Tathagata, the one who has come from reality." Verbal things are not the genuine spirit, and no matter how many Buddhist scriptures you read, and how many Buddhist names and forms you understand, this does not mean that you are sure to have the spirit of the Buddha. On the contrary, you must have the spirit to help living beings, and actually help living beings with your actions, and then you have the bodhisattva spirit. It does not matter whether or not someone is a disciple of the Buddha in form. For example, Tolstoy shared his land and farming equipment among the peasants, he abandoned his copyrights, and built schools. His goal was always to serve the people, to benefit living beings. At that time, he had a classic bodhisattva spirit.

Therefore it is said, do not get tied up by so many names and forms, do not deal with things and divide them up with the discriminating mind, do not rigidly adhere to forms. In all that you say and all that you do, just seek to benefit living beings and go toward the good. When you explain your faith, you must not calculate the results. Only then will you spontaneously become happy and free.

Bad Theories Are the Soil that Breeds Evil Deeds

When we measure a person's greatness, we shouldn't tonly judge in terms of a community or a nation. Rather, we must take the human race as the frame of reference, and look at whether or not the person has really brought something good to the human race. Of course, we also must measure this by taking all sentient beings, the earth, and the universe as a frame of reference. Some theories, though their point of departure may be good, have brought on violent atrocities, and made the world shed rivers of blood, and created enormous disasters for humanity. Such theories are definitely not good theories.

A friend asked me: "Many statesmen and philosophers have great character and want to benefit living beings — are they buddhas or not?" I told him that many statesmen and philosophers, when looked at superficially, have as their goal to benefit living beings, but they are not buddhas.

When we measure a person's greatness, we shouldn't only judge in terms of a community or a nation. Rather, we must take the human race as the frame of reference, and look at whether or not the person has really brought something good to the human race. Of course, we also must measure this by taking all sentient beings, the earth, and the universe as a frame of reference. Some theories, though their point of departure may be good, have brought on violent atrocities, and made the world shed rivers of blood, and created enormous disasters for humanity. Such theories are definitely not good theories. It doesn't matter whether or not their founders were good people. If it would be better not to have the theory than to have it, it is not a good theory. If we look at it from the point of view of the long flow of history and humanity, no matter how great the character of a theory's founder may have been, if the objective results brought on by that theory were disastrous, then the founder stands condemned through the ages as an evildoer.

There are cultures which, although they also have some good things, at the same time have evil things that are harmful to humanity, and may bring on such evils as warfare and vengeful killing. Then, no matter who has benefitted, from the point of view of humanity itself, they were all disasters. The Buddhist culture is one of peace.

Some philosophies, viewed objectively, have promoted evil. For example, some people think there is no spirit, so they indulge in unbridled corruption, pursuing worldly gain. Though some philosophies have been prominent for a certain period, in the long run of history, at best they have led humanity down crooked paths. If the human race as a whole would have been better off if these philosophies had not existed, they are bad theories. When you penetrate through the fog of history, and you see the basic substance, you will discover that the values which have been accepted by the great masses at any given moment were certainly not necessarily correct.

Therefore, with some theories, you do not have to look to see whether or not their founders ate meat, or whether or not their hearts melted when they saw beggars. If the things they transmitted created great misfortunes for humanity, then their minor virtues were not enough to cover their great evil.

The most deplorable thing in this era is that people with no grasp of the real truth go broadcasting their own so-called truth. These people are called philosophers or thinkers. If they are so short-sighted, they cannot see past their own noses. When they just see a tiny bit of light before their eyes, they think that they have grasped the truth of the universe, and they desperately proclaim this so-called truth, and make more people become short-sighted — objectively speaking, this is a kind of evil deed. This kind of evil deed is very scary. It is like a pestilence spreading to this world. So then, what is not an evil deed? It is when what you are spreading is a genuine truth. Though some people say there is no absolute truth, in fact there is an absolute truth — be of benefit to the whole human race and even to all living things. If a point of view does not benefit the whole human race, no matter how grand it might be, it is absolutely not the truth. Thus, truth must possess one basic criterion: goodness, that is, being beneficial to the whole human community, to all living spirits of this earth, and even to the whole universe.

There is a story in the Buddhist scriptures. A certain man thought that by killing more than a thousand people he would attain the Path. He thought this was the truth, and so he went everywhere killing people, and spreading this imagined truth. Though he wanted to have many people attain the Path, objectively speaking, this so-called truth of his could only bring disaster to other people. No matter what his original intention was, no matter how sincere he was, no matter how he put his whole heart and soul into it, his theory and his existence were evil. Thus, all violence is evil, all war is evil, all slaughter of humans is evil.

The weather is cool now, and there are many flies in my room — why don't I swat them? Because flies too are living things. In the space of this universe, a fly and I both have the right to live, and we possess this space in common, and I have no right to hurt it. But there is a theory that sees flies as a harmful insect, and would annihilate them. If I accepted this theory, my actions would surely be controlled by this theory, and so I would harm other forms of life.

This is why you must not only look at the subjective aspirations of a theory: you must also look at its objective results.

You must take humankind, history, and even the universe as the frame of reference to measure its worth.

I have never evaluated a person or point of view in terms of nation or community or ethnic group. Rather, I put it into a greater, more far-reaching frame of reference. For example, I have never considered Zeng Guofan (1811–1872, Qing Dynasty statesman and general credited with suppressing the Taiping Rebellion) as a great man—he was a butcher. The common people saw this clearly, so they called him "Shaven-Headed Zeng." Those who extol him certainly have the same butcher's gene as he did.

Can we say that if someone has killed many people, he is a great man? I do not consider Genghis Khan a great man. How can we say that because he killed so many people and wiped out so many countries, he was a hero? He was not. The true heroes are the people who do all they can to enable everyone to live a good life. Of course, Hong Xiuquan (1814–1864, a leader of the Taiping Rebellion, and thus Zeng Guofan's archenemy) was not a hero either. This pair of butchers competed with each other in slaughtering people, so it doesn't make sense to say either one of them was a hero.

I know that politicians would surely not agree with me. But no matter how strong the human race is, among the humans there always must be some people who understand this truth. If a learned person lacks this kind of thinking, lacks the spirit to benefit all of humanity, he is not any good as a learned person, he is just another living creature, the same as a fly.

Thus, we must leap beyond the environment of our own lives, and leap beyond the knowledge we have learned. We must stand high above humankind, above all living things, from flies to tigers, and reflect on this world. We do not only belong to a certain group, we do not even only belong to humanity as a whole.

There are also some people who think that to push history forward, it is necessary to rely on war and slaughter. But examined objectively, is history actually moving forward, or is it regressing? Of course, societies and economies have progressed, but the spirit and morality of people has steadily declined. Life has gotten more convenient, but the quality of life has been declining. So what does this imply?

A friend said to me that literature is powerless. It is truly powerless, but this apparent powerlessness is nevertheless forever powerful. For example, Emperor Wu of the Han Dynasty had power, and he had (the historian) Sima Qian castrated. At that time Sima Qian was quite powerless. But after Emperor Wu's physical body was gone, the power of Sima Qian became apparent: his thinking has influenced the masses for more than two thousand years. You tell me: was Sima Qian's immortal work *Annals of History* more powerful, or was Emperor Wu more powerful? The weakness of literature is temporary. This is because literature is something that transmits light, and this light does not only function in its own era, it also can illuminate the future. Its light is something very powerful, not something weak.

In human history many philosophers and thinkers have appeared, but those who have truly made an active contribution to the human race have been few. The contributions of many philosophers to humanity are far from being as great as the contribution of Jesus to humanity. If the lines of thinking proposed by some philosophers had been followed, the human race might surely have gone toward tyranny and given birth to many evil things. But when Jesus appeared, he caused people to understand universal love. When Kant appeared, he made the human race learn to respect itself more. Therefore, there are good philosophies and bad philosophies, and it is certainly not true that all philosophies have been beneficial to humankind. Some philosophies that have produced evil and violence have truly been terrible disasters for the human race.

Good and Evil Go Together Like Light and Darkness

The issue now is that an ocean of information is filling people's minds and spirits, but the media which control the information do not propagate a good spirit, or evoke a good orientation. Rather, with a total lack of principle, they meet the needs of the social order, and amplify the noises of desire. As soon as some voices of good emerge, they are immediately drowned out by the sounds of the noise. I call these morally lost media people "unscrupulous media people."

Some philosophers say that Western philosophy is dead, and theology is dead. In fact, the spiritual crisis created by the crisis of faith is an evil result created by theology dying. At present, theology has begun to come back to life, and things like faith and spirituality are reviving. This is because people discover that when material needs are constantly satisfied, people begin again to seek spiritual things. When a nation is very impoverished, the needs of the physical body come first. After survival needs are satisfied, spiritual needs reenter people's field of vision. These days, as the Internet becomes more and more universal, it has filled a great deal of space in people's lives, and made people unconcerned with thinking about metaphysical issues. But this stage of being controlled by the Internet is only one stage in people's lives. For example, many people who love going online are youngsters, but after they have gone through the years of being Internet geeks, they may start to ponder serious questions. When people are in their twenties, they may indulge in pleasure and be oblivious of everything else. When they reach thirty or forty, they have to squarely face the questions of human life. Why are most of the people who like my writings over thirty? The literary journal *Wenhui Bao* in the issue for January 4, 2005 published an article reviewing my full-length novel *Desert Hunters*, and the article said that my novel covered spiritual topics, and this is not often seen. Moreover, what is most lacking in the works of contemporary Chinese writers is spiritual content. Because they lack these spiritual things, readers will not buy them, and they become estranged from literature. The fact that some readers will buy any writiny by Xuemo provides us with some information.

The issue now is that an ocean of information is filling people's minds and spirits, but the media which control the information do not propagate a good spirit, or evoke a good orientation. Rather, with a total lack of principle, they meet the needs of the social order, and amplify the noises of desire. As soon as some voices of good emerge, they are immediately drowned out by the sounds of the noise. I call these morally lost media people "unscrupulous media people." As this kind of people become more and more numerous, there is a rising tide of "unscrupulous culture." When the unscrupulous ones are in the majority of our society, then "unscrupulous culture" becomes the mainstream culture. On one hand, the unscrupulous people need unscrupulous culture, and on the other hand, the people who sell unscrupulous culture need a market—the two sides are clamoring for each other, and so they bring about the empty and false noise that we see in front of us.

But as some intelligent people, thoughtful people, and people with consciences try to exert some influence and light the sparks of wisdom, there is bound to come a time when more and more people wake up. At present, many of the people with power and position and resources and money are all "unscrupulous," and so they will build this kind of unscrupulous culture. Even so, such a situation ultimately cannot last forever. In any period, there will always be a group of unscrupulous people. In (the famous sixteenth century novel) *Water Margin*, there are many unscrupulous people, but in the end that bunch of unscrupulous villains were like flies buzzing along in the emptiness—they did not leave a trace. What can leave a bequest in history are all related to culture. The spark of culture will ultimately continue.

In the history of human civilization, apart from political affairs, what is left is only culture and thought, and in this we cannot see any trace of the unscrupulous people. Nowadays, although there are many unscrupulous people, they will never be able to leave a trace. The continuity of humankind is this way: in any period there is always evil, there is always greed, there is always desire, but within the human race there are sure to be some people who try to steer humanity away from evil, and this part of humanity will continue to exist as long as the human race exists. In every era there are some of these saviors. But along with these saviors, in the same period there are sure to be some evildoers who can never be saved. Thus, the saviors and the evildoers will continue to exist together, just as a light will always be accompanied by darkness. Humankind cannot get away from doing evil, because desire is a nightmare from which humans cannot escape. When there are humans, there will be evil deeds, and when there are evil deeds, there will be people urging humankind to get away from evil, but living beings cannot all be saved. This is because when each person is born, there may be the seeds of evil deeds, and those innate desires will make the person become evil. In this dirty evil world, the spirit of Shakyamuni Buddha and Jesus appears exceptionally great. This is like a torch in a dark night—it can light the way for the journey of the human mind and spirit, but it is impossible for it to make the whole dark night become light. Humanity's darkness and light coexist: if there is light, there must be darkness, and if there is wrongdoing, goodness must appear.

This goodness might be the power of faith. Only by using the power of the goodness in faith can the souls of a portion of the human race be rescued. But this power will be very limited, because as everyone knows, indulging desires brings the body more pleasures than purifying the mind and reducing desires, and enjoying pleasures is more comfortable than practicing asceticism. When people observe it without wisdom, they may prefer enjoying pleasures, they may prefer greed, they may prefer indulging desires, they may prefer descending into corruption, too lazy to think about certain questions. That's why most of the human space is occupied by dispensable unscrupulous people. But although there are multitudes of these unscrupulous people, their energy in fact is very limited. Throughout the entire human history, what can be passed down may be the thoughts of a few thinkers, or the writings that contain such thoughts, or a few good books. On the other hand, after fifty or a hundred years, the unscrupulous people will be swept away, by the winds of history, like bugs or fallen leaves in a whirlwind. What is left behind is the kind of thing we are talking about.

Suppose there comes a day when faith has totally died out, and humanity no longer has the least bit of introspectiveness or reverence or yearning — then humanity will be going toward annihilation. This is because the human race and the planet both have a lifespan. According to the Buddhist theory, all things have four stages: formation, abiding, disintegration, and extinction, and nothing lasts forever. In ancient times, people were very plain and unaffected, but as material conditions improved and developed, people's desires became greater and greater. The more information science develops, the more it can stimulate people's desires and greed, and the human race will produce more and more greed and desire, and this will accordingly bring more and more suffering and wrongdoing. These things will be unconquerable if the human race only relies on the natural state of letting things take their own course — this is the point I made in my novel *Desert Hunters*. As the conflicts of greed among the herdsmen become more and more intense, in the end they destroy what they subsist on. If we keep on not examining ourselves, the ultimate fate of humanity will also be like this. What eventually destroys the human race will be the human race itself. As the earth has fewer and fewer resources left, with the destruction of faith, humanity's ever-increasing greed, and more and more external enticements, humanity will have a harder and harder time. If we do not set to address the root problem, the destruction of the human race will be certain.

Plant Great Love in the Field of the Mind

No matter how much good fortune humans have, this is no more than a good state of mind. If the good state of mind continues for one day, then this is one day of good fortune; if it extends for a month, then this is one month of good fortune; if it extends for a year, then this is one year of good fortune; if it extends for a lifetime, then this is one lifetime of good fortune. If every person in a group has a good state of mind, then this group is fortunate; if every person in a nation has a good state of mind, then this nation is fortunate.

At present there are many wars and disasters, all because the transmission of something very good has been lost in human civilization, or shall we say, because it does not occupy the mainstream position. What occupies the mainstream are all things that have to do with desires, bloody things, violent things, like the various games involving killing people and capturing cities and so on. These kinds of things continuously carry to humanity an evil suggestion of selfishness, and increase the desires, greed, and hatred in the inner mind of humans, and form a kind of collective unconsciousness, making the whole society think that this is right. For example, many people even now have not found out how Zeng Guofan won (the war against the Taiping rebels in the nineteenth century), and that this object of study always did three things: first, he killed people; second, he waged war; third, he plotted conspiracies. Why have so few people studied why Gandhi succeeded, why Tolstoy succeeded, and why within faith there are so many excellent things like universal love?

What is most fearful for the human race is not killing, but singing the praises of killing. If we page through Chinese history and world history, we discover that what humans pay homage to is precisely killing their fellow humans. The more people someone kills, the more he is recognized as a hero, like Genghis Khan, Napoleon, Alexander the Great, Zeng Guofan, and so on. This is the downfall of the whole human race, and it is also the evil deed of those who write history books and participate in literature.

Those who kill people surely can kill because they have their power base and are incited by desire. We must be clear that killing is evil, and thus condemn it, rather than praise it. Singing the praises of killing is more accursed than killing itself. This is because the one who does the killing will die in the end, whereas the culture that praises killing will be passed down, influencing generation after generation of people, planting the seeds of evil in the human mind and spirit, nourishing them and making them grow, and finally smashing the world. The one wielding a sword is sure to attract an opponent's sword, but what evil deeds finally bury is the human race itself.

Thus, literature that praises the violent ones is a poisonous tumor on the human mind and spirit, and we must excise it. We must tell people very clearly that Napoleon, who was so powerful, was not a hero, that Genghis Khan, "who destroyed forty countries," was not a hero, and that those so-called heroes praised by the human race for centuries were in fact butchers, and bearers of evil. The real heroes were people like Gandhi, Lao Zi, Confucius, and Mencius, people who brought the elixir of love to humankind and to history—only they are worthy of being extolled and praised by humanity.

Perhaps we cannot control power, and we cannot eliminate evil, but we can control our pens and our throats, and put forth a voice with a relative conscience. A gentle voice will surely be drowned out by the clamor of the age, but when thousands of throats put forth their voices together, they might awaken the souls wrapped up in nightmares. If generation after generation keeps making efforts like this, it may be possible for there to be more people who clearly understand what evil is.

Many times, even more despicable than the killers themselves, are the ones cheering them on. In the noise from the cheering crowd, minor killers become major tyrants. Of course, one thing they may do is to take that killing knife, which gets crazier and crazier the more they use it, and cut out the brains of those who are cheering for them. Our literature must no longer be a cheering squad for evil deeds. This is because history tells us that all those who sing the praises of evil deeds will end up becoming sacrificial victims of the evil deeds. As we face one killing knife after another in history, we must raise our voices — even if that brings on a killing knife — and vehemently shout out "That is evil!" When human beings go on calling this out generation after generation, the rag of evil will be thrown into the sewer, and yield to conscience and virtue.

What I explained in the novel *Spells of Xixia* is precisely this kind of worldview.

What genuinely benefits the whole human community is not something narrow, something based on desire, but rather a kind of universal love. What do we call small love? What do we call great love? Small love means at least being able to let your loved ones achieve a good state of mind. In reality, no matter how much good fortune humans have, this is no more than a good state of mind. If the good state of mind continues for one day, then this is one day of good fortune; if it extends for a month, then this is one month of good fortune; if it extends for a year, then this is one year of good fortune; if it extends for a lifetime, then this is one lifetime of good fortune. If every person in a group has a good state of mind, then this group is fortunate; if every person in a nation has a good state of mind, then this nation is fortunate. When your love brings this kind of good state of mind to the loved ones around you, and you can make them happy and pure, this is small love. When your love brings the whole human race inspiration, purity and clear understanding, this is great love.

In history there are many instances of love that has moved the world. For example, Jesus was not only so good to the disciples around him, or to a woman; rather, he recognized that all humanity was worth caring about and loving—this is great love. Gandhi was this way too, and he advocated "non-violent resistance." Whatever group he dealt with, he always treated them with the great universal mind. In the end, when he was shot down by an extremist, he still advocated universal love—this then is great love. Great love is beneficial for the whole human community. It is something that truly must be praised and transmitted.

To raise small love to the level of great love, we must carry out a process of spiritual refinement. In fact, every person is carrying out this kind of process every day. In other words, this is raising the human character to a higher level and remolding the spirit.

How then do you raise the human character to a higher level and remold the spirit? You must examine yourself, and yearn for it. Examining yourself is discovering your shortcomings; yearning is respecting and emulating a being greater than your own. This being is not necessarily a divine being—it could be a person, a type of spirit, or a kind of art. You hope to achieve a way of living in unity with that great being and getting close to it, and you dedicate all your actions to it—you do not just think about it—this kind of action is called cultivation.

The best cultivation is when you are able, as you deal with people and situations in daily life, not only to discover your own inadequacies and limitations, but also to take as a reference the human character of a great being—for example, the Buddha—and correct your own defects, and in the midst of life and work, elevate the level of your own character, and become a better person, more compassionate, more pure and awake. You also take what you have received—purity, clarity, happiness, the ideals and thoughts and culture and light that are beneficial to the world—and transmit it forward, hopefully enabling people to live more happily than they did yesterday. Of all forms of cultivation, this is the highest realm, and it is called "giving the Dharma," because it can bring a good beautiful culture to this world. Every person is the initiator of a chain of transmission. When you have this kind of self-examination and yearning for truth, countless people around you will become links in this chain. One of the countless links may also send forth a different sound and light, and the influence will slowly spread out, and the whole world may also slowly change.

Don't Expect Yourself to Be Able to Hold onto Flowing Water

The world itself is a giant dreamlike illusion. When you clearly understand this dreamlike illusion, and you do not grasp it or become attached to it, this is the conduct of a person of wisdom. If you want to take this dreamlike illusion and change it into something that is real, something that can be held onto, this is called "grasping the illusory as real"—this is the basic cause of human affliction. The biggest affliction of humankind is to think that in this world filled with uncertainty, one can find certainty.

One day my son Chen Yixin brought up a very good question. He asked me: "The Renaissance in Europe functioned as an enlightening stimulus for the economy, and it was because of the atmosphere of freedom in the Renaissance period that there could be the later development of science and technology, the appearance of new technology, and the greater spread of democratic thought. I feel that globalization is also a kind of progress. What I want to ask you is this: First, what face should Buddhism show in this so-called Age of the End of the Teaching, and this era of rapid economic growth? Second, is it possible for Buddhism to appear in philosophical and cultural forms, and in the future, how will they be linked to interchange with each other? Will Buddhism be able to elevate human welfare or not? This welfare I am speaking of includes economic progress. Because everyone is facing the greatest uncertainty, this is something people fear. We have no way of controlling our fate in life and future. Will Buddhist wisdom be able to achieve a breakthrough in the face of this uncertainty, and enable human knowledge to manifest a qualitative leap, and thereby elevate the level of the human spiritual world as a whole?"

I told him that this "uncertainty" is exactly the truth which Buddhist wisdom recognizes. The concept of "permanent" referred to in the phrase "all compound things are not permanent" is "certainty," and "not permanent" is "uncertainty." When you clearly understand this uncertainty, that implies that you have clearly understood a certain truth. When you clearly understand that this uncertainty is unavoidable, you will not go looking for some kind of certainty. When you clearly understand that this world is a giant illusion, you will not hope for it to change into something that is not a dreamlike illusion.

This is because, when you hope it will change into something that really exists and has its own inherent nature, this is called false thought, and it is a kind of ignorance. Here's an example. You clearly know that a roll drawn on a piece of paper is only a drawing, and so you will not expect it to be able to fill your stomach. In the same way, if you want to take a world filled with uncertainty and make it more certain. this itself is an enormous false thought.

In other words, the world itself is a giant dreamlike illusion. When you clearly understand this dreamlike illusion, and you do not grasp it or become attached to it, this is the conduct of a person of wisdom. If you want to take this dreamlike illusion and change it into something that is real, something that can be held onto, this is called "grasping the illusory as real" — this is the basic cause of human affliction. The biggest affliction of humankind is to think that in this world filled with uncertainty, one can find certainty. Buddhist wisdom is telling people that this world is fundamentally illusory and impermanent, and we must not cling to it.

It's like what goes on between lovers. A boy asks a girl: "Do you love me or not?" The girls says: "I love you." When he asks her again tomorrow, the girl says: "I don't love you." The boy then asks: "Yesterday you said you loved me. How can it be that today you don't love me?" The girl says: "Yesterday was yesterday, today is today."

This girl understands very well that for a moment yesterday she did indeed love him. But as it turned out, after this moment passed, her state of mind changed, and so she no longer loved him.

When she had the state of mind of love, of course she loved you; when her state of mind changed, of course she did not love you. How can you demand that her state of mind definitely should not change?

The way people think when they are in a certain state of mind is like a bubble, suddenly appearing, suddenly gone. If you want to grab hold of this bubble, and keep it from changing, this is impossible. The most easily changed thing in the world is the human mind. The human mind is very easily changed, and feelings of love are also very easily changed. Thus, many people seek a love that will last forever, but this is almost impossible. Of course, within this, there is a kind of relative stability: when two people have a very good karmic connection, and strength of character enables the two people to accept each other, they can establish a relatively stable connection in marriage. But even this is not something that lasts forever. This is because all people are moving toward death, and death will always separate the people who love each other.

A married couple will of course seek to grow old together, but ultimately will they be able to do so? The uncertain factors in this world are many. For instance, if one suddenly chokes and dies as a result, then there will be no way for him to grow old together with his beloved one. No matter why it happens, if your heart stops beating, you won't be able to grow old together with your spouse. After you go out the door, if you run into a car whizzing by, there will be no way to grow old together. If some of your cells become cancerous, and they are not detected by your immune system, it is also likely that you won't be able to grow old together.

This is why we say that everything is fundamentally empty and illusory. The world is empty and illusory, and even the many experiences of meditation are empty and illusory. They are suddenly born and suddenly extinguished, and go through myriad changes every moment. When we clearly understand this empty illusion and do not cling to it, this is liberation. If we do not clearly understand this empty illusion, and we are unwilling to accept it as empty illusion, and thus always want to cling to it, this is suffering.

Why has Buddhist wisdom continued to exist over millennia? What will it rely upon to continue to exist in the future? What is the meaning of its existence? Well, it exists for people to see through empty illusion, to enjoy the present moment, to be awake in the present moment, and to clearly understand the present moment. It exists to enable people to understand the real characteristic of the world.

When you can directly experience that everything is like a dream, like an illusion, you will know very clearly that this world itself is a gigantic illusion, and everything is no more than a dream, and all external forms are the coming together of causes and conditions.

When you genuinely accept the empty illusory unreality of the world, you understand that whether you want it or not, whether you accept it or not, everything is changing every moment, and you do not care about these things. Of course, when you have not yet seen the real characteristic of the world, you still do care about it. When stocks go up, you are so happy that you can't express it; when stocks fall, it hurts so much that you can't pull yourself out of it. This is because you do not know that booming or crashing, stocks have no necessary connection to the essential body of your life, because they cannot fundamentally change anything about you.

Nothing in the external world can fundamentally change anything about you. What can change you is your mind. When the mind changes, everything changes. If the mind does not change, nothing changes. When a millionaire living in a luxurious house is suffering and jumps to his death, basically he is as fortunate as a homeless guy who sleeps in the street. For many wealthy people, when they are approaching death, their colossal wealth becomes a totally meaningless number, and their sons and daughters may get into a life-or-death struggle to take their wealth. They have worked hard their whole lives only for the sake of some numbers that have no absolute connection to themselves — you tell me, ultimately, is there any meaning in this?

Afterword:

What Is a Genuine Disciple Like?

A Talk on Learning and Practice

These two books, *The World Is a Reflection of the Mind*, and *Let Your Mind Belong to Yourself*, are a popularization of the Mahamudra philosophy that I advocate. Originally, I had not planned to put out such books. The reason was that I was afraid of wasting everybody's time. There are many viewpoints, and in fact I had already explained them. But because the books I had written previously had a lot of religious terminology, the average person might not like them, and so Chen Yanqin proposed that I write a book for people who do not necessarily have any religious faith. This was the origin of the present book.

I have already written a full account of my point of view in the book itself, and I will not repeat myself here. Now, I just want to speak of the connection between learning ideas and putting them into practice.

Krishnamurti had a sense of loss in his later years. He discovered that, even though he had been propagating the truth for several decades, there was not a single person who really practiced what he preached. That is to say, he had many readers and students, but no disciples. This was of course related to the great break within his family. He went a bit too far in "breaking up appearances," and broke off connection between himself and his lineage of teachers. He threw out the baby with the bathwater. It is like what I spoke of in *The Holy Monk and the Spirit Woman*: "The basic substance of faith is yearning. The objective which can make you yearn for it must be something which cannot be treated with disrespect." The "break" between Krishnamurti and his family, though glorious, was a case where going too far was like not going far enough. The fact that he also broke with his own lineage of transmission is one of the basic reasons that he had no disciples in the true sense of the term.

There is also a great master of Buddhist culture who acknowledged that he had students, but no disciples.

Thus, someone asked me about the difference between students and disciples. I answered that for students, the emphasis is on learning and knowledge, while for disciples, the emphasis is on action and putting things into practice. The former are students; the latter are students too, but more than that, they are practitioners.

In the teaching of the Kagyu Shangpa tradition, there are many kinds of disciples: disciples who form a karmic connection with the teacher, disciples who take refuge with the teacher, disciples who act according to the teaching, disciples who go up to the teacher's hall, disciples who enter the teacher's room, disciples who get the transmission of mind, and so on. In fact, disciples who form a karmic connection with the teacher and disciples who take refuge with the teacher are not disciples in the strict sense of the term; only after they act according to the teaching do they count as disciples. That is to say, between disciples and teachers, apart from the required ritual forms, the most necessary thing is in fact action. Every time Shakyamuni Buddha expounded a sutra, his disciples would then all "accept it faithfully and carry it out respectfully." Only someone who "accepts it faithfully and carries it out respectfully" is a true disciple.

The biggest distinction between disciples and students lies in this: students emphasize intellectual knowledge, while disciples emphasize wisdom. Wisdom can lead to wondrous function, and that wondrous functioning will become manifest in their actions. Without action, there is no wisdom. If there are a lot of people who follow a certain teacher and listen to his lessons, but they do not work hard to apply the lessons in their actions, naturally they are not disciples. Disciples in the traditional sense study the teachings, transmit them, put them into practice, respect them, receive the bequest of wisdom, and even more, they rely on their teacher in their actions—none of these factors can be missing. For students, on the other hand, if they can read books and study, that is good enough.

For this reason, in the traditional Shangpa culture, concrete demands are placed upon "disciples who act according to the teaching." If we use contemporary language to explain these, there are about nine items:

1. Enter deeply into one gate (This is the tradition's "one teacher, one teaching, one fundamental buddha.")

2. Every day, do at least one session of yoga meditation practice. (When the disciple is on a retreat, do four sessions of yoga every day.)

3. Every week, do at least one activity to spread the teaching (like reading at a meeting, or some other form of transmitting the teaching).

4. Every month, do one ceremony of making offerings. (The twenty-fifth day of the month on the lunar calendar is the birthday of the Vajrayogini.)

5. Every half year, participate in some events for the common good of society, and be of service to society.

6. At least once every year, do a summary evaluation of your cultivation and practice.

7. At least once every year, take part in a lecture forum or a meditation forum, and study intellectual knowledge.

8. Establish your own method for spreading the teaching.

9. Always participate in activities to spread culture that is of benefit to the collective common good.

These nine items are my up-to-date contemporary explanations of the practices of the traditional Shangpa Kagyu School. The purpose is to enable the knowledge which you have studied to be transformed into your own wisdom. The effectiveness of any kind of learning is very limited if it cannot be reflected in our actions and our way of living. I met an old teacher who lectured on Buddhist culture: although he had written many things, the expression on his face was gloomy, and he looked annoyed, and he spoke in a contentious way — obviously, though he may have cultivated the Buddhist Path, it had not transformed his mind. I wonder if what he has learned is meaningful for his life. If your studies cannot even save yourself, then how can you save the world? This is why, in the traditional Buddhist culture, there are concrete requirements for disciples. Those who are interested can go read the book *Fifty Verses on the Teachings of Master Teachers*.

Because of this, if I have disciples, they are not just people who "study" intellectual knowledge with me. Rather, they are people who join in "putting it into real practice" with me. This real practice includes: studying intellectual knowledge, cultivating the realization of wisdom, refining the human character, transmitting culture, continuing the lineage of transmission, spreading the truth, benefitting living beings with their actions, and so on. As for all those people who have just gotten a bit of intellectual knowledge from my books, or have learned a bit about cultivating contemplation — if they are not "sharing in the cultivation" by putting it into real practice, then they are not my disciples. Thus, students are easy to get, but disciples are hard to find. Bodhidharma (the First Zen Patriarch in China) sat facing a wall for nine years, and only then did the Second Patriarch come. In this world there is no shortage of pretentious talkers, but what we need are people who get the job done quietly without attracting attention.

The reason I emphasize "putting it into real practice" here, is that now we must let ourselves take the books we have read, and use them to transform our actions. I likewise hope that those people who read my books will take the knowledge in these books and put it into actual practice, and use their action to complete their own genuine reading, and let the wisdom of the Great Mudra become the way they themselves live their lives. Only this kind of reading has meaning. This is also where the system of "Great Mudra Yoga" differs from the usual fast-food reading material.

图书在版编目（CIP）数据

世界是心的倒影 = The World Is a Reflection of the Mind：英文 / 雪漠著；（美）柯利瑞（J.C.Cleary）译. 一北京：中国大百科全书出版社，2018.5

ISBN 978-7-5202-0273-2

Ⅰ.①世… Ⅱ.①雪… ②柯… Ⅲ.①散文集-中国-当代-英文

Ⅳ.①I267

中国版本图书馆CIP数据核字（2018）第088033号

出 版 人　刘国辉

特约编审　阿去克

策划编辑　李默耘

责任编辑　姚常龄

特约编辑　弓秀英　刘　彦

英文校对　石学亮

责任印制　邹景峰

封面设计　U-B**OO**K

出版发行　中国大百科全书出版社

地　　址　北京阜成门北大街 17 号

邮　　编　100037

网　　址　http://www.ecph.com.cn

电　　话　010-88390739

印　　刷　北京市十月印刷有限公司

开　　本　880 毫米 ×1230 毫米　1/32

字　　数　99 千字

印　　张　9.5

版　　次　2018 年 5 月第 1 版第 1 次印刷

定　　价　65.00 元

本书如有印装质量问题，请与出版社联系调换